Play Fair! Play Smart!

Who needs a cheat code when you're playing to win? What you really need is a game plan to unlock rare items and attain impressive achievements in video games—that's what this book is all about!

Whether you own a Nintendo Wii, Xbox 360, Sony PlayStation 3, or Nintendo DS, you'll find plenty of tips for locating obscure items, unlocking tough achievements, and winning big in multiplayer contests. You'll find information about a variety of game situations on a wide selection of titles, including tips for the beginnings, middles, and ends of your favorite video games.

Before you turn the page to find your favorite games, keep a few things in mind:

DLC Happens

Some game titles featured in this book may receive additional downloadable content (DLC), which means there's a small chance that some of the information and conditions for unlocking items or achievements could change in the future—but that's a very small chance.

Consult Your Console

Xbox 360 Gamerscore Achievements and PlayStation 3 trophies might be featured on games with identical titles, but these awards are not always identical. For example, PlayStation 3 trophies include a platinum trophy for unlocking all the trophies in a game, but you usually won't find a similar Gamerscore Achievement for Xbox 360 games. To avoid confusion, be sure to consult the correct achievement award lists for your game console(s).

Win Awards Fast

In some games, we highlighted specific Xbox 360 Gamerscore Achievements and PlayStation 3 trophies because there's a trick or handy strategy to earning those awards. If you want to maximize your awards with only a few hours of game play, check out those sections first.

Set Reasonable Goals

Some of these challenges take many hours of game play. You're obviously not going to win the "It Takes Time (HR)" Bronze Trophy in a single night of playing MLB 09: The Show on the PlayStation 3, so start with reasonable goals—like winning the Bronze Trophy for stealing three bases in one Road to the Show game.

Use this guide to unlock the biggest challenges in today's video games, and remember —have the fun along the way!

TABLE OF CONTENTS

A
B
C
D
E
F
G
H
I
J
K
L
M
N
O
P
Q
R
S
T
U
V
W
X
Y
Z

ADVANCE WARS: DAYS OF RUIN
NINTENDO DS

Commanding Officer Unlocks

While you start Advance Wars: Days of Ruin with four capable Commanding Officers, you'll eventually find some highly skilled leaders as you push past Chapter 11. Here is a list of the available COs and how to unlock them in Campaign mode:

CO	Boost or Specialty	Unlock Conditions
Tasha	Air units/Sonic Boom	Complete Chapter 12: History of Hate
Gage	Naval and artillery	Complete Chapter 13: Greyfield Strikes
Forsythe	5-square command zone	Complete Chapter 14: A Hero's Farewell
Waylon	All air units	Complete Chapter 20: Waylon Flies Again
Greyfield	Naval, seaplanes, 'copters	Complete Chapter 21: Lin's Gambit
Penny	Stormfront weather control	Complete Chapter 24: Crash Landing
Tabitha	Firestorm attack	Complete Chapter 25: Lab Rats
Caulder	5 HP recovery to units	Complete Chapter 26: Sunrise

ANIMAL CROSSING: CITY FOLK
NINTENDO WII

The Catch of the Day That Pays!

Does a Black Bass sell for more than a Clownfish? Most Animal Crossing anglers fish until their inventory is full, but If you know how much a fish is worth, you can keep the stuff that sells for the most Bells! This practical list can help you catch and keep the most valuable fish, giving you a whopping profit when you sell them to Tom Nook!

Fish	Bells
Angelfish	3,000
Arapaima	10,000
Arowana	10,000
Barbel Steed	200
Barred Knifejaw	5,000
Bitterling	900

continued...

800

Tom Nook
When a fish takes the bait, the floater will sink, and you must pull up with good timing!

Fish	Bells
Black Bass	300
Blue Marlin	10,000
Bluegill	120
Butterflyfish	1,000
Carp	300
Catfish	800
Char	3,800
Cherry Salmon	1,000
Clownfish	650
Coelacanth	15,000
Crawfish	250
Crucian Carp	120
Dab	300
Dace	200
Dorado	15,000
Eel	2,000
Football Fish	2,500
Freshwater Goby	300
Frog	120
Gar	6,000
Giant Snakehead	5,500
Goldfish	1,300
Guppy	1,300
Hammerhead Shark	8,000
Horse Mackerel	150
Jellyfish	100
Killifish	300
King Salmon	1,800
Koi	2,000
Loach	300

I caught a dab!

And I'm feeling fab!

continued...

Fish	Bells
Lobster	2,500
Moray Eel	2,000
Napoleonfish	10,000
Neon Tetra	500
Octopus	500
Olive Flounder	800
Pale Chub	200
Pike	1,800
Piranha	2,500
Pond Smelt	300
Popeyed Goldfish	1,300
Puffer Fish	240
Rainbow Trout	800
Ray	3,000
Red Snapper	3,000
Salmon	700
Sea Bass	160
Sea Butterfly	1,000
Sea Horse	1,100
Sea Sunfish	4,000
Shark	15,000
Squid	400
Stringfish	15,000
Surgeonfish	1,000
Sweetfish	900
Tuna	7,000
Yellow Perch	240
Zebra Turkeyfish	400

continued...

Tip: *So where and when can you catch the most valuable fish? Your best chances for finding the Stringfish are in the river during twilight and evening hours throughout December, January, and February. The Coelacanth can be found in the sea all year in the twilight and evening hours—but you can only catch the fish when it is either raining or snowing!*

Don't Let Earning Bells Bug You!

While chasing down bugs and butterflies for Bells is fun, you'll find it more profitable if you know the value of the Bells in your net. The list below will show you how much a bug is worth so you can fill your inventory with the most worthwhile catches in the game!

Bug	Bells
Common Butterfly	90
Agrias Butterfly	3,000
Bee	4,500
Yellow Butterfly	90
Raja Brooke	2,500
Long Locust	200
Tiger Butterfly	160
Birdwing Butterfly	3,000
Migratory Locust	600
Peacock Butterfly	220
Moth	60
Mantis	430
Monarch Butterfly	140
Oak Silk Moth	1,200
Emperor Butterfly	1,200
Honeybee	100
Orchid Mantis	2,400
Brown Cicada	200
Robust Cicada	300

continued...

Bug	Bells
Walker Cicada	400
Evening Cicada	550
Lantern Fly	1,800
Red Dragonfly	80
Darner Dragonfly	200
Banded Dragonfly	4,500
Giant Petaltail Dragonfly	8,000
Ant	80
Pondskater	130
Diving Beetle	800
Snail	250
Cricket	130
Bell Cricket	430
Grasshopper	160
Mole Cricket	280
Walking Leaf	600
Walkingstick	600
Bagworm	300
Ladybug	200
Violin Beetle	260
Longhorn Beetle	260
Dung Beetle	600
Firefly	300
Fruit Beetle	100
Scarab Beetle	6,000
Jewel Beetle	2,400
Miyama Stag Beetle	1,000
Saw Stag Beetle	2,000
Giant Beetle	10,000
Rainbow Stag Beetle	10,000

continued...

Bug	Bells
Cyclommatus Beetle	8,000
Golden Stag Beetle	12,000
Dynastid Beetle	1,350
Atlas Beetle	8,000
Elephant Beetle	8,000
Hercules Beetle	12,000
Goliath Beetle	6,000
Flea	70
Pill Bug	250
Mosquito	130
Fly	60
Centipede	300

Bug	Bells
Spider	300
Tarantula	8,000
Scorpion	8,000

Tip: *The most valuable insects are the rare Hercules Beetle and the Golden Stag Beetle, which sell for 12,000 Bells each. These beetles are only found very late in the evenings through early mornings in July and August. While the Golden Stag Beetle likes ordinary trees, the Hercules Beetle prefers palm trees. It's not uncommon to find only one of these beetles a year!*

ANIMAL CROSSING: WILD WORLD
NINTENDO DS

How Can I Help Tom Nook Expand His Store?
Tom Nook remodels and expands his store depending on how many Bells you spend. Expanding the store allows Tom to sell a large variety of merchandise. Here are the remodeling guidelines:

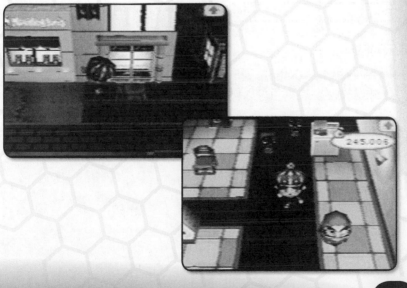

Store	What to Do
Nook 'n' Go	Spend at least 25,000 Bells
Nookway	Spend at least 90,000 Bells
Nookington's	Have a friend link to your town and visit Nookway, then spend at least 240,000 Bells.

How Do I Earn Golden Items?

Some golden items are easier to earn than other items. The Golden Shovel is usually the first gold item that new players collect.

Golden Item	How to Earn It
Golden Axe	Trade a Scallop shell with Pascal (he's on the beach once a week)
Golden Bug Net	Catch one of every bug in the game
Golden Fishing Rod	Catch one of every fish in the game
Golden Slingshot	Knock 15 items out of the sky with your slingshot, and then shoot down the Golden Slingshot
Golden Shovel	Bury a normal shovel and then dig it up 24 hours later. If you waited long enough, you'll uncover the Golden Shovel
Golden Watering Can	Weed and water your surroundings and if you keep it perfect for 16 consecutive days, you'll earn the Golden Watering Can from Pelly or Phyllis.

Where Do I Find the Scallop Seashell?

Trading items in Animal Crossing: Wild World is the only way you'll earn the Golden Axe from Pascal, but the trading steps are complicated and it takes a little time. The first step is to buy a Red Turnip from Joan.

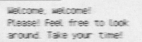

Trade This	To	For This
Red Turnip	Wendel	Turban or Country Guitar
Turban	Sahara	Massage Chair or Red Vase
Massage Chair	Tortimer	Scallop Shell

If you get the Country Guitar or Red Vase, you must return to Joan for another Red Turnip for Wendel, but you can still trade for other rare items.

Trade This	To	For This
Country Guitar	K.K. Slider	K.K. Picture
Red Vase	Redd	Safe
Safe	Tom Nook	Tom Nook Picture

AVATAR: THE LAST AIRBENDER: THE BURNING EARTH

XBOX 360

An Easy 1,000 Points!

Avatar: The Last Airbender: The Burning Earth offers an opportunity to earn 1,000 Gamerscore Achievements in one minute, which makes it the absolute must-have for Gamerscore point farmers. You can earn your points in the first area of the first level, but the trick is knowing where to stand.

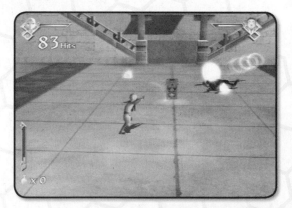

The First 300 Points

Start in Chapter 1, stand near the center of the courtyard, and press B until you defeat all the guards. This should earn you The Flow of Combat I and The Flow of Combat II achievements before the general talks to you. That's 300 points!

I am General Fong, leader of this Earth Nation base. We've been expecting you, Avatar Aang!

It's All About the B Button

After the general calls in more troops, the game will direct you to use your combo attacks with the X Button and it will teach you how to block by using the RB Button—but keep pressing the B Button instead!

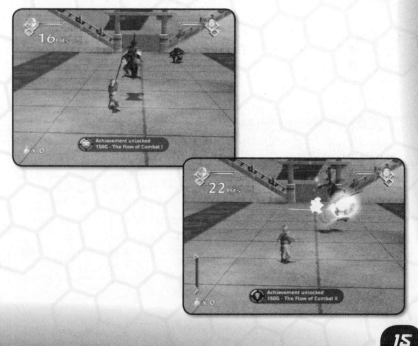

By using only your B Button on these attacks, you'll advance your Hit Counter to a maximum of 50 in less than a minute of game time.

The trick is to avoid being hit while constantly hitting the B Button. If you're hit by one of the guards or hurt in any way, your hit counter will go back to zero and you'll have to start over again!

You'll find it easier to increase your Hit Counter if you target and knock back the guards closest to you first, and then keep them all at a distance. If you accomplish this, you'll earn The Flow of Combat III, The Art of Combat, and the One with Combat achievements in roughly one minute! Remember to use the B Button—no other buttons!

Avatar: The Last Airbender: Burning Earth Gamerscore Achievements

Achievement	How to Earn It	Points
The Flow of Combat I	Achieve a hit counter of 10	150
The Flow of Combat II	Achieve a hit counter of 20	150
The Flow of Combat III	Achieve a hit counter of 30	200
The Art of Combat	Achieve a hit counter of 40	200
One with Combat	Achieve a hit counter of 50	300

BOOM BLOX

NINTENDO WII

Blast Away These Bonus Unlocks!

You can use these unlocked items in Create mode. If you're having trouble determining which Explore mode levels unlock items, look for question marks revolving around certain stages—that's where you need to play!

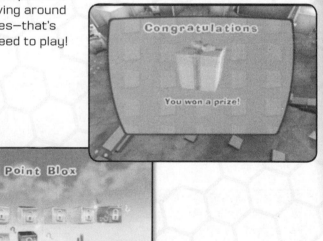

Item	Unlock Conditions
Bomb Ball	Earn at least a Bronze Medal at Box Stax "More Flying Bombs" in Explore mode
Bowling Ball	Earn at least a Bronze Medal in Gem Blox "Boulder" in Explore mode
Cloud Blox	Earn at least a Bronze Medal in Gem Blox "FinE Art" in Explore mode
Coconut	Earn Gold Medals on all Tiki Rescue levels
Eight Ball	Earn Gold Medals on all Medieval Sneaky Thieves levels
Fire Hose	Earn at least a Bronze Medal in Chemical Blox "Line Up" in Explore mode
Firework Blox	Earn at least a Bronze Medal in Bomb Blox "Weak Wall" in Explore mode
Fragile Blox	Earn at least a Bronze Medal in Vanish Blox "Three Flat" in Explore Mode
Ice Blox	Earn at least a Bronze Medal in Chemical Blox "Green Gush" in Explore mode
Laser	Earn at least a Bronze Medal in Point Blox "Plumber" in Explore mode

Item	Unlock Conditions
Laser Hose	Earn Gold Medals on all Adventure Challenge levels
Nuke Bomb	Earn Gold Medals on all Explore Challenge levels
Rubber Ball	Earn at least a Bronze Medal in Vanish Blox "Towering Fries" in Explore mode
Racquetball	Earn Gold Medals on all Tiki Crossing levels
Shotgun	Earn Gold Medals on all Western Bandit Blast levels
Six Shooter	Earn Gold Medals on all Western Blastin' Site levels
Skull Ball	Earn Gold Medals on all Haunted Lost Kitten levels
Tennis Ball	Earn at least a Bronze in Grab Tool "Sparkplug" in Explore mode
Vanish Point Blox	Earn at least a Bronze in Point Blox "Cannon Clash" in Explore mode.

More Explore Mode Challenges!

You can unlock these challenging Explore mode stages by completing the following:

Expert Explore Challenges	Earn Silver Medals in all Explore mode challenges
Master Explore Challenges	Earn Gold Medals on all Explore mode challenges

BURNOUT: PARADISE

XBOX 360 AND PLAYSTATION 3

Find the Parking Garages!

You can find the repair shops, gas stations, and junkyards on your in-car GPS map, so why can't you find the parking garages? Most parking garages take you up to higher elevations, where you'll find stunt ramps and passages to boosts, billboards, and other cool secrets. Whenever you see a sign with a Yellow "P" for parking garage, hit the e-brake and head into the lot. Drive to the top of the parking buildings, and you might take your billboard-bashing scores to higher levels!

Are You Missing Super Jumps, Billboards, or Smashes?

Tracking down the last Super Jumps, Billboards, and Smashes in Burnout Paradise can be as tough as mastering your Burnout Elite License, but there is a handy menu that can help you find what you're missing.

+ Pause your game and go to the Burnout Paradise Network.
+ Click on the Stats tab, and then click on the Discovery button.*
+ The Discovery Menu breaks down your Super Jumps, Billboards, and Smashes according to five areas in the game—Palm Bay Heights, Downtown Paradise, Harbor Town, White Mountain, and Silver Lake.

*Depending on your console, you might have to press the X Button on the PS3 or the A Button on the Xbox 360 controller to "click" on an item in this menu.

Road Warrior Tips for Road Rage Mode in Paradise City

If you race enough, you'll realize that driving through a gas station along a course can top-off your boost rating so you can use it for more speed. This same strategy works with the Repair Shops in Road Rage mode—you can increase your vehicle's endurance by driving

through a Repair Shop in Paradise City during the event. You can only drive through a Repair Shop for repairs ONCE during the Road Rage event, so save your Repair Shop stop until the colors on your screen fade almost to black-and-white (the scenery around you loses color as your car strength runs out).

Maintain Your Speed

While most players know to choose the strongest Aggression car from their Junkyard inventory, some slow down too much during the event (especially when making sharp turns) and this makes their cars an easy target for rival ragers bent on destruction. Speed is just as important as car strength for the final Takedown challenges in the game.

Burnout: Paradise Xbox LIVE Gamerscore Achievements

Achievement	How to Earn It	Points
Lookin' Good	Repair your car	5
Watt?	Establish a Time Road Rule on Watt Street	10
It's Showtime	Set a Showtime Road Rule on East Crawford Drive	10
Great Race	Win a race	10
Misdemeanor	Smash through five billboards	10
Off the Beaten Path	Earn 25 smashes	10
Perfect Rage	Earn 10 takedowns in Road Rage without a wreck	5
Rising from the Ashes	Repair a Damage Critical condition during a Road Rage event	10
Spinnin' Around	Execute a 360-degree spin	10

Achievement	How to Earn It	Points
Learning to Fly	Land five super jumps	10
Duckin' and Weavin'	Win a Marked Man challenge without a takedown	10
All Pimped Out	Win all Burning Routes in the game	10
Explorer	Find all events in the game	10
Online Racer	Complete an online race	10
First Win	Win an eight-player online race	10
Shopaholic	Find all drive thrus in the game	10
Party Crasher	Complete 25 online challenges	15
Happy Snapper	Send your mug shot out five times using your Xbox Live Vision camera	10
Join the Party	Complete one online challenge	10
Just for Pics	Take down your first online rival	10
Bottom of the Class	Earn your Class D license	20
The Show Must Go On	Earn an x10 multiplier in Showtime mode	20
Rampage!	Earn a Takedown Rampage	20
Parallel Park	Parallel park with a 100% rating score	20
Supercharged	Win 25 Burning Routes	20
Car in a China Shop	Earn 500 Takedowns in the game	20
Paid and Displayed	Smash through all parking lot barriers in the game	20
Bustin' Out	Smash through all billboards in the game	20
Totally Smashed	Collect all smashes in the game	20
Flying High	Land every super jump	20
Speed King	Earn a Time Road Rule on every road	20
Crashin' All Over the World	Earn a Showtime Road Rule on every road	20
Online Champion	Win ten online races	20

Achievement	How to Earn It	Points
Notorious	Send 50 mug shots via your Xbox Live Vision camera to other players	20
Criterion Elite	Earn your Elite License, win all events, and find everything	20
Firestarter	Take down 50 different gamers online	20
Hotshots	Earn 50 snapshots in your lineup	20
Criterion Fever	Take down one of the Burnout Paradise developers	20
DareDevil	Land a two-rotation barrel roll jump	25
Boosting Around the World	Earn an x20 Boost Chain	25
Millionaire's Club	Score over a million points in Stunt Run mode	25
Party Animal	Finish 250 online challenges	20
Underachiever	Earn your C Class License	30
Online and Kicking	Complete 20 online events	30
Burnout Skills	Top six of the "Today's Best Scores" in 8-player online freeburn mode	30
Block Party	Excluding the PDLC, finish a whole section of online challenges	40
Must Try Harder	Earn your B Class License	40
Flying Colors	Earn your Class A License	50
Paradise Won	Earn your Burnout Driving License	60
Elite	Earn your Burnout Elite License	70

PS3 Trophy List

Action	Trophy
Repair your car	Bronze
Set a Time Road Rule on any road	Bronze
Set a Showtime Road Rule on any road	Bronze
Win a Race	Bronze

Action	Trophy
Smash 3 Burnout Billboards	Bronze
Smash 30 Burnout Billboards	Bronze
Drive through 10 sets of Yellow Smash Gates	Bronze
Shut down the Nakamura SI-7	Bronze
Score an x3 Multiplier in Showtime	Bronze
Perform 3 Takedowns	Bronze
Drive through a Repair Shop in Road Rage	Bronze
Perform a 180-degree Flatspin	
Successfully land your first Super Jump	Bronze
Perform a Burnout Chain of x2	Bronze
Survive a Marked Man	Bronze
Beat the target score in Stunt Run	Bronze
Power Park your car	Bronze
Set ten Showtime Road Rules	Bronze
Set ten Time Road Rules	Bronze
Complete five Burning Routes	Bronze
Drive on the wrong side of the road for 547 yards	Bronze
Shut down the Carson Inferno Van	Bronze
Land ten Super Jumps Successfully	Bronze
Land a Barrel Roll Jump	Bronze
Find all the Events in Paradise City	Bronze
Invite a friend to join you in Paradise City	Bronze
Complete a Freeburn Challenge	Bronze
Visit a Gas Station during a Race	Bronze
Visit a Paint Shop to change your car's colors	Bronze
Enter a Road Rage event in the Carson Inferno Van	Bronze
Visit the Airfield	Bronze
Visit the Quarry	Bronze
Jump Dead Man's Edge	Bronze

A
B
C
D
E
F
G
H
I
J
K
L
M
N
O
P
Q
R
S
T
U
V
W
X
Y
Z

Action	Trophy
Jump over another Player's Car	Bronze
Complete ten Freeburn Challenges	Bronze
Eight players meet in the Wildcat's Baseball Stadium	Bronze
Send a mug shot (Smugshot) to a player	Bronze
Take part in an Online Stunt Run event (Cagney Expansion)	Bronze
Take part in an Online Marked Man event (Cagney Expansion)	Bronze
Be on the Blue Team for an Online Road Rage event (Cagney Expansion)	Bronze
Be on the Red Team for an Online Road Rage event (Cagney Expansion)	Bronze
Ride 50 miles offline on a bike (Bike Expansion)	Bronze
Complete any Bike Day Road Rule event (Bike Expansion)	Bronze
Complete any Bike Night Road Rule event (Bike Expansion)	Bronze
Ride ten miles on a bike in an eight-player lobby (Bike Expansion)	Bronze
Complete 5 Bike Challenges (Bike Expansion)	Bronze
Drive 750 miles	Silver
Score over 50,000 points in a Stunt Run	Silver
Perform a Burnout Chain of x4	Silver
Drive through 200 sets of Yellow Smash Gates	Silver
Score an x5 Multiplier in Showtime	
Earn your "D" Class License	Silver
Earn your "C" Class License	Silver
Earn your "B" Class License	Silver
Earn your "A" Class License	Silver
Complete your first Timed Challenge (Cagney Expansion)	Silver

Action	Trophy
Complete 24 hours of game time on a bike (Bike Expansion)	Silver
Earn your 'Burnout" Driving License	Gold
Smash 60 Burnout Billboards	Gold
Complete 10 Timed Challenges (Cagney Expansion)	Gold
Earn 100% complete with your Bike License (Bike Expansion)	Gold
Burnout Paradise Elite Platinum Trophy	Earn all trophies in the game

CARCASSONNE

XBOX 360

Want to Lead in Multiplayer? Watch the Followers!

If you want to be a leader in Carcassonne games against the computer or other players, focus on where other players place their follower/meeple pieces. Playing your follower/meeple pieces late in the game can help you win huge points, especially in farmlands. You can also trap other players' follower/meeple pieces and limit their ability to win points at the end of the game. Here are some of the best traps:

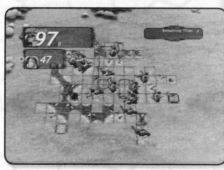

Unfinished Towns

Players often drop their follower/meeple pieces inside town walls, but if you extend and expand the width of these walled areas (especially with complicated pieces that include town walls and a road), your opponents will have a tougher time completing their walls and they'll lose a follower/meeple in the unfinished construction.

Unfinished Roads

Players who place a follower/meeple on a road must complete both ends of the stretch with an intersection, a town gate, or a monastery. If you pick up an end-piece for a road, don't place it where your opponent can use it and gain extra points. Focus on making your own road or creating a faraway detour that your opponent can't use for points.

Unfinished Monasteries/Cloisters

You can't score points for a follower/meeple inside a monastery/cloister unless you can surround the structure with eight square tiles, that's why most players with a monastery/cloister tile try to place the building next to a group of tiles already on the board. If your opponent places a follower/meeple inside a monastery/cloister, don't help them finish construction. Just surrounding a monastery/cloister halfway requires four turns, and that's four turns where your opponent must focus on placing tiles in one spot while you build and add extra points in other areas on the board.

Don't Create Huge Pastures

Followers on big open spaces score the most points in the game, but a follower/meeple sent to pasture can't be retrieved. If your opponent places a follower/meeple in a pasture, quickly close off the plot with city walls and roads. On Carcassonne's easy difficulty, you'll find that the computer player doesn't use follower/meeple in farmland, so you should take advantage of these extra points before placing the final tiles.

Know the Odds for Important Tiles

As you play more games, you'll notice that there are a finite number of tile pieces and configurations. Later in the game, you'll be able to guess which tiles will be drawn if you remember how many of these important tiles are in the deck:

+ Four tiles feature a three-way intersection.
+ Three tiles feature a three-way intersection next to a city wall.
+ There are three city gate tiles but only two of these tiles feature shields.
+ Four monastery/cloister tiles are surrounded by pastures.
+ Two tiles feature a monastery/cloister at the end of a road.
+ There is only one tile featuring a four-way intersection.

Tip: *Counting the intersection pieces on the board and knowing how many are left in the deck makes it easy to trap your opponent's follower/meeple pieces on roads late in the game! And doing the extra math can make it easier for you to score the most points in a game!*

Carcassonne Xbox LIVE Gamerscore Achievements

Achievement	How to Earn It	Points
Mirror Monk	Complete two monasteries/cloisters side-by-side in single-player mode	25
King of the Road	Complete a road with a follower/meeple and five or more tiles in single-player mode	5
Rack up the Points	Earn at least 50 points in single-player mode	10
Farm Boy	Complete a farm that supplies at least four completed cities in single-player mode	10
Big City	Complete a city that covers at least three or more tiles in single-player mode	5
King for a Day	Win an Xbox LIVE ranked match	15
Top Score	Score at least 2,000 points in all Carcassonne games combined	15
Top of the Heap	Win in Player Match mode against three or more opponents	20
The Count of Carcassonne	Score at least 150 points in single-player mode	20
Metropolis	Score a city that covers nine or more titles in Player Match mode against two or more opponents	25
Lord of Carcassonne	Defeat a Player Match mode opponent by at least 50 points	25
Ultimate Score	Score at least 5,000 points in all Carcassonne games combined	25

The Best Trick for Unlocking Great People in a Hurry

The secret to unlocking all of the Great People in the game is to raise your culture level through culture bonuses. Select the Romans or the Greeks for your civilization—they have a small bonus for attracting Great People. Make your task easy by choosing the easiest difficulty level (Chieftain, so you can avoid attacks) and playing the Beta Centauri scenario. This scenario starts with all technology, so you can focus on maxing out your rating culture. Switch your government style to Monarchy to add to this cultural bonus, and then build structures like courthouses, temples, and cathedrals that add cultural value.

Tip: If you select the Greeks for your civilization, you'll automatically start with a courthouse. Later in your game, you can add the Magna Carta wonder to your courthouse for an additional cultural bonus.

Once your culture is growing rapidly, choose a challenging wonder so the game progresses without interruption until you have all the Great People unlocked!

Civilization Revolution Xbox LIVE Gamerscore Achievements

Achievement	How to Earn It	Points
One mistress and no master	Win as the English	15
I will not be triumphed over	Win as the Egyptians	15
Flower and song	Win as the Aztecs	15
A short life of glory	Win as the Greeks	15

Achievement	How to Earn It	Points
Fair and softly goes far	Win as the Spanish	15
Blood and iron	Win as the Germans	15
Veni, vidi, vici	Win as the Romans	15
A great wind is blowing	Win as the Russians	15
Let a hundred flowers bloom	Win as the Chinese	15
We the people	Win as the Americans	15
Imagination rules the world	Win as the French	15
An indomitable will	Win as the Indians	15
A knight without fear or blame	Win as the Arabs	15

Achievement	How to Earn It	Points
This world is a harsh place	Win as the Africans	15
All others must fail	Win as the Mongolians	15
Victory over lesser men	Win as the Japanese	15
Difficulties mastered	Win a victory using each civilization in the game	30
A revelation of man	Win a Cultural Victory	20
Embiggens, the smallest man	Win a Cultural Victory on King difficulty level or higher	30
Citizen of the world	Win a Cultural victory on the Deity difficulty level	45
Have fun storming the castle	Win a Domination Victory	20
Vi victa vis	Win a Domination Victory on King difficulty level or higher	30
Such joy ambition finds	Win a Domination victory on the Deity difficulty level	45
A penny saved is a penny earned	Win an Economic victory	20
The guy who signs the checks	Win an Economic victory on the Deity difficulty level	30
Playing the game	Win an Economic victory on the Deity difficulty level	45
Ideas control the world	Win a Technology victory	20
640K ought to be enough	Win a Technology victory on the King difficulty level or higher	30
Indistinguishable from magic	Win a Technology victory on the Deity difficulty level	45
Destroyer of worlds	Win a Victory of every type (Cultural, Domination, Economic and Technology	30
The universal brotherhood of man	Develop a city that produces 200 culture per turn	25

Achievement	How to Earn It	Points
Organized knowledge	Develop a city that produces 200 science per turn	25
The root of all evil	Develop a city that produces 200 gold per turn	25
Curse of the drinking class	Develop a city that produces 200 resources per turn	25
Buy the ticket, take the ride	Make contact with another civilization	3
Culture is worth a little risk	Build a Wonder of the World	9
Once more into the breach	Combine three units into an army	5
80% of success is showing up	Unlock a famous person by accumulating culture	5
Home is where one starts from	Construct a special building	3
Good afternoon, Doctor Jones.	Discover an ancient artifact	9
Before all else, be armed	Develop a special unit ability for combat	5
Scientia potentia est	Develop and complete any technology	3
Napalm in the morning	Defeat an enemy unit	3
The fruit of labor	Build a second city (using a Settler) in a game	5
What is the city but the people?	Expand a City to size 20	25
The will to win is everything	Win 20 battles with a single unit	25
Here's looking at you, kid	Unlock all famous people in the game	45
That we may live in peace	Win a game by year 1000 A.D. on King difficulty or higher	25

Achievement	How to Earn It	Points
Absolute power is kind of neat	Win without making a government change on King difficulty or higher	25
Power never takes a back step	Win on at least King difficulty level while only founding one city	25

CLUB PENGUIN: ELITE PENGUIN FORCE
NINTENDO DS

I'm an Official Elite Penguin Force Agent! What Do I Do Now?

The beginning of the fourth mission can be a little confusing. Try these moves:

+ After you receive your badge, talk to the director.

+ Grab the file from the table and show the documents to Dot.

+ Give the file to the penguin behind the counter in the Sport Shop, and he'll give you Gary's glasses.

A
B
C
D
E
F
G
H
I
J
K
L
M
N
O
P
Q
R
S
T
U
V
W
X
Y
Z

+ Use Gary's glasses at the Eye Scan 3000 machine next to the locked Gadget room door.

+ Explore the room and then click on the drawer. Inside, you'll find the Mechno-Duster.

+ Take the Mechno Duster to the top of the chairlift and use it to blast away the object in the snow.

+ Take the bent key.

+ Go back and talk to Dot, and then use the key on the door!

COLLEGE HOOPS 2K6

XBOX 360

Create a Maxed-Out Player

Set the play mode to Simulation and drop the difficulty level to Starter. You can probably earn 700 Gamerscore Achievements in one game if you create a player with maxed-out abilities and maximize the game length.

College Hoops 2K6 Gamerscore Achievements

Get 45 Rebounds with Any Team   **200 points**

Fire shots from the three-point line with your newly customized star player. If you're playing with a highly rated team, there's a good chance they'll catch a lot of offensive rebounds.

Make 15 Three Pointers in One Game
250 points

This feat is easy if you feed the ball to your customized star player. It also helps if you turn off player fatigue and verify that you're playing with the longest possible game time in Simulation mode.

Score 40 Points With Any Player
250 points

If you're feeding your star player the ball and he's shooting from the three-point line, you'll nail this feat with the one above.

Get 20 Steals With Any Team
150 points

Set the game time to the maximum allowed for each half and be sure to choose a team that's rated high (about five basketballs on the graph) for Defense. Use the Right Analog Stick to strip the ball, but keep in mind that your team will probably be called for more fouls than in most games. Remember, you're looking for a 20-steal total for the entire team, not a single player.

Get 6 Blocks with Any Player
150 points

At the Game Sliders option on the Options menu, max out the Block Attributes on Defense. (Otherwise, you must time your block with your customized star player and knock the ball back without creating a foul.)

If you're still fouling out, go to Rules on the Options menu and turn off Goaltending. Then push the Left Block and Reaching Fouls sliders to zero. If that doesn't work, allow the computer players to block for you by keeping the best defensive players on the court throughout the entire game.

Best Opponents

While choosing a good team isn't a big problem in College Hoops 2K6, finding the easiest teams to beat can take some work. Here are the best opponents to play for Gamerscore achievements (conferences are in parenthesis to help you find these teams):

+ Savannah St. (IND)
+ Princeton (IVY)
+ Morgan State (MEAC)
+ Army (Patriot)
+ Grambling (SWAC)
+ MD. Eastern Shore (MEAC)
+ Kennesaw St. (A-SUN)
+ Alcorn State (SWAC)

- + North Florida (A-SUN)
- + Stony Brook (AEC)
- + Colgate (Patriot)
- + UC Davis (IND)
- + Mississippi Valley State (SWAC)
- + Prairie View (SWAC)
- + Brown (IVY)
- + Howard (MEAC)
- + C. Michigan (MAC)
- + Lehigh (Patriot)
- + Alabama State (SWAC)
- + Arkansas-Pine Bluff (SWAC)
- + Dartmouth (IVY)
- + Mount St. Mary's (NEC)
- + Idaho (WAC)
- + VMI (Big South)
- + Yale (IVY)

DIRT

PLAYSTATION 3, XBOX 360

Translating Pacenotes

Although rally racing is popular throughout the rest of the world, North American race fans don't get to see much of it on television. This can make it hard to figure out the pacenote directions your co-driver is giving you when you're racing in the Rally and Rally Raid stages.

Here are the translations:

"60 left five" means that the curve 60 meters ahead turns left and can be taken in 5th gear.

Depending on road surface and weather conditions, you'll find that you don't have to brake at all on turns that are rated for 6th and 5th, and possibly 4th, gears, unless your driver says:

"80 right four tightens." This means that the curve 80 meters ahead turns right and should be taken in 4th gear—and the corner will seem sharper toward the end. If the course is narrow and you manage to gain a lot of speed in the 80 meters before the turn, it's probably a good idea to tap the brakes, especially if there isn't a guardrail to keep you on the racecourse.

On technical courses, your co-driver will give you several course instructions at once:

"Jump into left four, right three" means that there is a jump, followed by a 4th-gear left turn and then a 3rd-gear, right turn. In this case, you must be ready to tap the brakes as you land after the jump, but the quick left-right turn combination might be enough to lose speed without forcing you to hit the brakes.

Watch That Crest!
Because you can't see everything on the course, learn to trust your co-driver's pacenotes, especially when you hear the term "at crest." There's a good chance an upcoming hill will block your view of what's ahead. Also, recognize that any "crest" will be a "jump" in the pacenotes if you're driving fast enough.

Say what? Later in the game, you'll encounter technical courses with lots of blind turns and fast bends, so your co-driver's pacenotes might sound a little confusing until you have more practice. If you're feeling confused, just listen for the gear numbers in the pacenotes. Be ready to brake if you hear a number three or lower.

Going Up!

As in other rally video games, it's important to remember that the pacenote readings for gear choices around turns are guidelines. As you advance into the higher tiers, you must push the limits of your car and take turns in higher gears to win first place. Because the Rally Raid trucks move slower and require more time to accelerate, you'll find that you can navigate some course turns much faster than the gears recommended by your co-driver—especially going uphill. But in most cases, you'll still brake for any pacenote turn with a "one" or "two" in it.

Dirt Xbox LIVE Gamerscore Achievements

Achievement	How to Earn It	Points
Driven in excess of 100 miles	Drive 100 miles in Career mode	5
Driven in excess of 250 miles	Drive 250 miles in Career mode	10
Driven in excess of 500 miles	Drive 500 miles in Career mode	20
Driven in excess of 1,000 miles	Drive 1,000 miles in Career mode	25
Tier 2 career points milestone	Earn the maximum points through all of Tier 2 in Career mode	10
Tier 4 career points milestone	Earn the maximum points through all of Tier 4 in Career mode	10
Tier 6 career points milestone	Earn the maximum points through all of Tier 6 in Career mode	20
Tier 8 career points milestone	Earn the maximum points through all of Tier 8 in Career mode	20
Maximum career points milestone	Earn the maximum points through all eleven tiers in Career mode	45
FWD rally veteran	Win all FWD Rally events in Career mode	20
4WD rally veteran	Win all 4WD Rally events in Career mode	20

Achievement	How to Earn It	Points
Classic rally veteran	Win all Classic Rally events in Career mode	20
RWD rally veteran	Win all RWD Rally events in Career mode	20
Rallycross veteran	Win all Rallycross events in Career mode	20
Rally raid T1 veteran	Win all Rally Raid T1 events in Career mode	20
Rally raid T4 Truck veteran	Win all Rally Raid T4 Truck events in Career mode	20
CORR super buggy veteran	Win all CORR Super Buggy events in Career mode	20
Hill climb veteran	Win all Hill Climb events in Career mode	20
Hill climb big rig veteran	Win all Hill Climb Big Rig events in Career mode	20
Crossover veteran	Win all Crossover events in Career mode	20
Champion of Champions winner	Win the Champion of Champions event in Career mode	20
National Rally veteran	Win all National Rally events in Career mode	20
Own 15 vehicles	Own 15 vehicles in career mode	15
Own 30 vehicles	Own 30 vehicles in career mode	30
Own All vehicles	Own all vehicles in career mode	45
First podium finish	Earn a podium finish (1st, 2nd, or 3rd) in any game mode	15
First victory	Win a race in any game mode	15
Hat trick—three wins in a row	Win three consecutive races in any game mode	15
5 wins	Win five races in any game mode	10
10 wins	Win ten races in any game mode	15

Achievement	How to Earn It	Points
20 wins	Win twenty races in any game mode	20
First 20-meter jump	Clear 20 meters in the air on any game mode	15
First clean race	Complete a race without hitting any cars or course markers in any game mode	15
Manual transmission	Win a race using the manual transmission setting in any game mode	10
Top speed	Exceed 135 MPH during any race event in any game mode	10
All tracks	Race on all tracks in any game mode—but not shakedown stages	20
First Xbox LIVE rally win	Win a ranked rally race on Xbox LIVE	20
First Xbox LIVE hill climb win	Win a ranked hill climb race on Xbox LIVE	20
First Xbox LIVE clean race	Avoid colliding with any car or obstacle in a ranked race on Xbox LIVE	20
Win Shell Rally Australia	Win the Shell Rally Australia in Championship Mode	20
Win Sparco Rally Espana	Win the Sparco Rally Espana in Championship Mode	20
Win Bremo Rallye Italia	Win the Bremo Rallye Italia in Championship Mode	20
Win Rally Deutschland	Win the Rally Deutschland in Championship Mode	20
Win BP Ultimate Rally UK	Win the BP Ultimate Rally UK in Championship Mode	20
Win Arai Japanese Alpine Rally	Win the Arai Japanese Alpine Rally in Championship Mode	20

Achievement	How to Earn It	Points
European Rally Champion	Win the European Rally Championship	25
International Rally Champion	Win the International Rally Championship	40
Global Rally Champion	Win the Global Rally Championship	60

DRAGON QUEST IV: CHAPTERS OF THE CHOSEN
NINTENDO DS

Fungeon Secrets
After you finish the main story in Dragon Quest IV, you can take your party to the Fungeon through the hole next to the King in Azimuth, but don't attempt this until you're at level 41 or higher.

At the end of the Fungeon, you'll find a pair of bosses named Chow Mein and Foo Yung. Because Foo Yung can cast revive spells on Chow Mein, it's important to target this spellcaster first. Focus on using buff spells on your party. Borya should cast Accelerate (and Sap) while Kiryl uses Kabuff.

After you defeat this duo the first time, you can return to Pinnacle Chapel and fight your way back to these monsters. Before the battle, you'll see a picture of a soldier. Each time you defeat Chow Mein and Foo Yung, you'll win an item in the picture. But as the boss

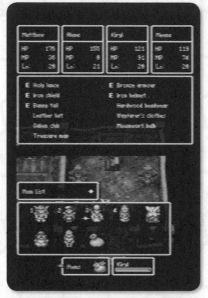

battle progresses, you'll have less time to defeat these two, so it's important to finish the fight as fast as you can. Here are the rewards:

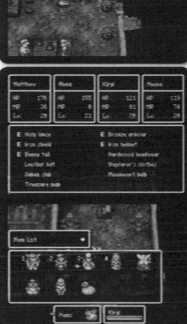

Second Battle Reward	Pandemonic Shield
Third Battle Reward	Pandemonic Sword
Fourth Battle Reward	Pandemonic Armor
Fifth Battle Reward	Boxer Shorts
Sixth Battle Reward	Yggdrasil Leaf
Seventh Battle Reward	Old Man Psaro

To win the seventh battle, you must defeat both Chow Mein and Foo Yung in nine rounds or less!

FERRARI CHALLENGE
XBOX 360, PLAYSTATION 3

How to Unlock Cars

There's more than one way to unlock cars in Ferrari Challenge, but most gamers use these Trophy mode races to roll away these steeds from the prancing horse. Here's the complete list of cars and conditions for winning in Trophy mode:

Car	Game Condition
Ferrari FXX	Win the Oro Trophy
Ferrari F50	Win the Bronzo Trophy
Ferrari F430 GT2	Win the Carnelian Trophy
Ferrari F40	Win the Bronzo Trophy
Ferrari F355 Berlinetta	Win the Perla Trophy
Ferrari 7333 SP	Win the Argento Trophy
Ferrari 575M Maranello	Win the Malachite Trophy
Ferrari 550 Maranello GT	Win the Tourmaline Trophy
Ferrari 512 S	Win the Opale Trophy

Car	Game Condition
Ferrari 365 GTB/4	Win the Obsidian Trophy
Ferrari 360 Modena	Win the Perla Trophy
Ferrari 360 GT	Win the Topaz Trophy
Ferrari 250 TestaRossa	Win the Rubino Trophy
Ferrari 250 LM	Win the Platino Trophy
Ferrari 250 GTO	Win the Zaffiro Trophy
Ferrari 348 TB	Place at least third or better at Misano in the Italian Challenge
Ferrari 348 Challenge	Complete the Monza event in the Italian Challenge
Ferrari F355 Challenge	Win at Paul Ricard in the Italian Challenge
Ferrari 575 GTC	Complete Arcade mode on easy settings
Ferrari 512 M	Complete Arcade mode on medium settings

PlayStation 3 Trophies

Trophy	How to Earn It
100 Wins Bronze Trophy	Win 100 races in any mode
2000 On the Clock Bronze Trophy	Cover 2000 miles in racing and qualifying
Double Whammy Bronze Trophy	Win two podiums in the European Challenge
Euro Lap King Bronze Trophy	Set new lap records for all European Time Trial tracks
First Across the Line Bronze Trophy	Finish first on every track in the game
First Challenge Win Bronze Trophy	Win a race in the Italian Challenge
Hot Shot Bronze Trophy	Earn at least 75% in all Tutorial mode categories
Italian Lap King Bronze Trophy	Set new lap records for all Italian Time Trial tracks
Numero Uno Bronze Trophy	Earn pole position through qualifying for an Italian Challenge race
Prancing Horse Bronze Trophy	Finish the Italian Challenge series
The Collector Bronze Trophy	Unlock all cars in the game
The Graduate Bronze Trophy	Finish Tutorial mode
The Veteran Bronze Trophy	Complete Arcade mode on expert settings
Trofeo Acciaio Bronze Trophy	Win the F575 Maranello Tournament
Trofeo Argento Bronze Trophy	Win the F40 Tournament
Trofeo Bronzo Bronze Trophy	Win the F575 GTC Tournament
Trofeo Carnelian Bronze Trophy	Win the F360 Modena Tournament
Trofeo Diamante Bronze Trophy	Win the F250 GTO Tournament
Trofeo Diasparo Bronze Trophy	Win the F550 Maranello GT Tournament
Trofeo Ferro Bronze Trophy	Win the F348 TB Tournament
Trofeo Granato Bronze Trophy	Win the F333 SP Tournament

Trophy	How to Earn It
Trofeo Malachite Bronze Trophy	Win the F550 Maranello Tournament
Trofeo Merurio Bronze Trophy	Win the F430 GT2 Tournament
Trofeo Obsidian Bronze Trophy	Win the FXX Tournament
Trofeo Opale Bronze Trophy	Win the F365 GTB4 Tournament
Trofeo Oro Bronze Trophy	Win the F50 Tournament
Trofeo Perla Bronze Trophy	Win the 355 Challenge Tournament
Trofeo Platino Bronze Trophy	Win the F512 M Tournament
Trofeo Rame Bronze Trophy	Win the F348 Challenge Tournament
Trofeo Rubino Bronze Trophy	Win the F512 S Tournament
Trofeo Smeraldo Bronze Trophy	Win the F250 Tessarossa Tournament
Trofeo Topaz Bronze Trophy	Win the F355 GTB Tournament
Trofeo Tourmaline Bronze Trophy	Win the F360 GT Tournament
Trofeo Zaffiro Bronze Trophy	Win the F250 LM Tournament
Unlock and Roll Bronze Trophy	Unlock a Tournament car
US Lap King Bronze Trophy	Set new lap records for all US Time Trial tracks
Euro Racer Silver Trophy	Win a race on every track in Europe
Italian Stallion Silver Trophy	Finish the Italian Challenge with maximum points
The Champ Silver Trophy	Complete Arcade mode on Legend setting
Time Trial Lap King Silver Trophy	Set new lap records for all tracks in the game
US Race Ace Silver Trophy	Win a race on every track in the North American Challenge Circuit
American All-Star Gold Trophy	Finish the North American Challenge with maximum points
Arcade Gold Gold Trophy	Earn a gold trophy for each level of arcade difficulty

A
B
C
D
E
F
G
H
I
J
K
L
M
N
O
P
Q
R
S
T
U
V
W
X
Y
Z

Trophy	How to Earn It
Circuits Maximus Gold Trophy	Finish the European Challenge with maximum points
The Perfectionists Gold Trophy	Earn 100% completion for the entire game
Congratulations Platinum Trophy	Unlock all trophies in the game

FIFA 06: ROAD TO WORLD CUP
XBOX 360

A Perfect Solution to a Big Achievement Challenge

Winning a match on Perfect difficulty might seem like the toughest 50 Xbox LIVE Gamerscore Achievements you could earn in any game. Here's a trick that some experienced players use to get around it:

+ Create a new Friendly Match and pair a favorite strong team like Germany or England against a weaker team like Liechtenstein. Choose Liechtenstein as your team and set the half-length to two minutes (the minimum) and the difficulty level to Perfect.

+ Watch the time carefully and be sure to let the team playing against Liechtenstein take the lead.

+ Wait until the last minutes of the second half—85 minutes is a good goal—then pause the game, choose Match Options and Select Sides.
Switch your controller from Liechtenstein to the strong opponent game—and don't let Liechtenstein win!

+ Depending on how much time you have left in stoppage, you might find yourself fighting off a couple of shots from Liechtenstein (at the Perfect difficulty level this tiny team is a formidable foe). Do your best to keep the ball and use long passes (press the X Button) to clear the ball from your end. If you can hold off the assault, you'll pick up 50 Xbox Gamerscore Achievements in less than five minutes of actual playing time!

Balls, Uniforms, and Legendary Team

Unlockable Item	Condition
Classic 11 Team	Qualify for the World Cup in Road to the World Cup mode
England 1990 kit	Win the International Open in Road to the World Cup mode using England

Unlockable Item	Condition
England 1996 kit	Win the International Masters in Road to the World Cup mode using England
France 1998 kit	Win the International Open in Road to the World Cup mode using France
Adidas Etrusco Ball	Win against at least eight teams in a customized Knockout Tournament
Adidas Tango Espana Ball	Win against at least 16 teams in a customized Knockout Tournament
Adidas Tricolour Ball	Win against five teams in Team Custom League play

FIFA 06 Xbox LIVE Gamerscore Achievements

Achievement	How to Earn It	Points
Qualify for the FIFA World Cup	Qualify for the World Cup through Road to FIFA World Cup mode	300
Win World Masters	Win the World Masters tournament in Road to FIFA World Cup mode	200
Win International Open	Win the International Open in Road to FIFA World Cup mode	200
Win Custom Knockout	Win a Custom Knockout made from at least eight teams	100
Win on Perfect	Win a match using the Perfect difficulty mode setting	50
Win a Custom League	Win Tournament mode using a custom league	150

FIFA 07

XBOX 360

A Winning Man of Match Achievement Strategy

Strikers tend to score more than midfielders and defenders, but you must play smart to win the Man of the Match awards 50 times for all three positions. Most FIFA 07 gamers have no problem earning the Man of the Match award for their strikers because the game usually awards the Man of the Match award to either the best goal scorer (a striker) or a goalie with a clean sheet (no one scored against him). But there is one proven trick: Swap your strikers for midfielders for the midfielder Man of the Match award, and then swap your strikers and midfielders for defenders for the defender Man of the Match award.

Even if your defender is playing forward in a new role, the game will still record his Man of the Match award as a defender. The challenge is finding good defenders who can also score goals. Phillip Lahm, John Terry, and Fabio Carnnavaro are all easy picks as defenders who can score goals and win Man of the Match awards.

FIFA 07 Xbox LIVE Gamerscore Achievements

Achievement	How to Earn It	Points
Winning Streak	Earn a 60-game winning streak on semi-professional difficulty	90
10 Goal Match Wonder	Score more than ten goals in a match on semi-professional difficulty	100
300 Game Winner	Win at least 300 games combined in all game modes and on any difficulty level	200
Defender Man of the Match	Win the Man of the Match award for a defender at least 50 times in semi-professional difficulty	50
Midfielder Man of the Match	Win the Man of the Match award for a midfielder at least 50 times in semi-professional difficulty	50
Striker Man of the Match	Win the Man of the Match award for a striker at least 50 times in semi-professional difficulty	50
Goal Getter	Earn an average of four-goals per game for at least 50 games in semi-professional difficulty	50
Undefeated	Earn an undefeated record for at least 50 games in semi-professional difficulty	50
World XI Master	Win at least 20 games using the World XI at the professional difficulty level	80
Fair Play Award	Play at least 20 games without earning a yellow or red card in semi-professional difficulty	100
Undefeated Manager	In Manager mode, keep your team undefeated throughout an entire season in any league and on any difficulty setting	200

125 Quick and Easy Xbox LIVE Gamerscore Points!

Earning triple-digit FIFA Gamerscore points normally requires hours of gameplay, but with a little careful planning and a lot of simulating, you can win 125 Gamerscore points without setting foot on the pitch. Here's what you do:

+ Go to Game Modes.
+ Choose Tournament Mode, and then Create Tournament.
+ Choose Knockout and put the Number of Teams at 64.
+ Select "NO" for Auto Fill Teams.
+ Now, choose your opponent teams.

This is time-consuming, but it takes much less time than attempting to win a 64-team tournament with the computer sorting for you.

+ Find teams for your tournament with one star or less. You can also choose a number of these one-star teams as your personal team, but make sure that they have an ATT rating near 60. Some of the worst half-star teams in FIFA 09 can be found in leagues in Ireland, in

A
B
C
D
E
F
G
H
I
J
K
L
M
N
O
P
Q
R
S
T
U
V
W
X
Y
Z

England's Coca-Cola Leagues, or in The Rest of the World rankings.

+ After you find all the half-star teams, fill up the remainder of the spots with one-star teams from small, underpowered leagues in Poland, Sweden, Austria, Australia, Switzerland, the Czech Republic, and Germany's 2. Bundesliga.

+ After you assign all of the one-star and half-star teams to tournament slots, save your file, so you don't have to sort through 64 teams for this achievement again.

+ Choose a good team for yourself, or if you want to make things a bit challenging and play a bit, you can choose one of the strong one-star contenders from the list below.

Tip: *If you don't choose the winning team the first time you simulate the tournament, you can return to your saved files and hopefully pick winners who advance beyond the group stages!*

Strong one-star
contenders include:
+ Sønderjyske
  (Denmark SAS Ligaen)
+ Tescoma Zlin (Czech
  Republic Cescka Liga)
+ Shrewsbury (England
  Coca-Cola League 2)
+ AFC Tubize (Belgium
  Pro League)
+ SCR Altach (Austrian Bundesliga)
+ Peterborough (England Coca-Cola League 1)

Once you have 50 Gamerscore points from your 64-team
custom tournament, go back and select the following:

+ Go to Game Modes
+ Choose Tournament Mode, and then Create Tournament
+ Choose Knockout and put the Number of Teams at 16
+ Select "NO" for Auto Fill Teams

Repeat the same team assignments, but select up to 15 half-
star computer-controlled teams from Ireland or England's Coca-
Cola Leagues. Choose one-star teams for yourself (any of the
strong one-star contender teams listed above will work fine).
Remember that you can win these 75 Gamerscore points as long
as one of your selected teams wins the tournament!

FIFA 09 Xbox LIVE Gamerscore Achievements

Achievement	How to Earn It	Points
1st Time out	Win a match in Online League	10
A. Bell Fever (Secret)	Catch A. Bell Fever by beating the creator or someone who has it	20
A man down	Win a game while down a man	20
Bend it like a pro	Score in a match with a free kick	15
Club god	Earn Legendary Status for your club	40

Achievement	How to Earn It	Points
Custom sixty-four winner	Win a Created Tournament with 64 teams (Use Knockout)	50
Director in the making	Upload a video to EA Sports Football World	10
Duo-Hedgeidecimal (Secret)	Enter a match with 20 other players in FIFA 09 Clubs Match	50
Eat my chip	Score by chipping over the keeper during a match	10
FIFA fair play (Secret)	With bookings enabled, play five consecutive matches without receiving a card	40
Fling yourself at it	Score using a diving header in a match	20
Frequent flyer	Win a match in every stadium	20
Giant killer	Defeat a five-star rated team using a half-star rated team	15
Gimme five (Secret)	Score five goals in the arena while the game loads (cumulative)	5
Good head on your shoulder	Score a header during a match	10
Hero	Save a Penalty Shot	10
Huge investment	Buy a player in Manger Mode for 50 million	20
Huge return	Sell a player in Manger Mode for at least 50 million	30
In off	Score off the woodwork (post) in a match	20
Jonzo's Lounge (Secret)	Score 2,500 points and win five badges in a single Lounge Mode match	60
Judas (Secret)	Beat your favorite team while playing as their rival	10
Last gasp goal	Score in the 89th minute of a match	19

Achievement	How to Earn It	Points
Like on the training field	Score from a corner	10
Living legend	Reach Legendary status for your country	50
Manual labor	Win a match in full manual settings (no assistance on)	10
On the spot	Score from a penalty in a match	5
On yer bike!	Score from a bicycle kick	30
One goal a season	Score using a defender during a match	10
One-star winners	Win a 16-team custom tournament using a one-star rated team	75
Optimus Chung (Secret)	Win a game with Adidas Live Season enabled	10
Pictures speak a thousand words (Secret)	Upload five screenshots to EA Sports Football World	10
Provider	Perform a cross for a multiplayer friend who scores from it	10
Ranked winner	Win a Ranked Xbox LIVE match	10
Real world winner	Win at least five Interactive League matches	20
Screamer!	Score from 30 yards out during a match	10
Sparkly clean (Secret)	Keep a clean sheet in a game	10
Spending spree	Buy at least 50 players during your Manager Mode career	20
The Gipson Curse (Secret)	Enter an online match after choosing your own arena player	10
The Kwong (Secret)	Score a header with the shortest created player possible	10
The ol' wwitcheroo (Secret)	Perform a pass that switches the play from one flank to the other	5

A
B
C
D
E
F
G
H
I
J
K
L
M
N
O
P
Q
R
S
T
U
V
W
X
Y
Z

Achievement	How to Earn It	Points
The Parolin Maneuver (Secret)	Win a game while not signed into Xbox LIVE	10
The Peterson (Secret)	Play FIFA 09 for over 50 hours	1
The Poon Sang (Secret)	Win using eleven created players on Xbox LIVE	20
The Purist	Complete a season in Manager Mode without simulating a game	100
The Venhola Ice (Secret)	Win a FIFA 09 Clubs match using your club	20
Time you played a match? (Secret)	Score twenty goals in the load-game arena	15
What a beauty!	Score from a volley in a match	5
Wing play	Score on a cross play in a match	10

FORZA 2 MOTORSPORT
XBOX 360

Earn Extra Funds without Spending Extra Time Behind the Wheel

Extended Endurance races might seem like a long haul, but starting at level 20, you can use the Hire Driver option to buy your way into these races. This technique can earn you thousands of game credits in FORZA2 Motorsport—without actually playing the game!

Although good drivers charge you about 60% of your winnings (don't pay more than that unless you don't want to pay for car upgrades), you can earn more than thirty thousand credits for a race that you don't have to drive!

Tip: *Joystick Trick*
There is one trick you should know before heading down this expressway to easy profits—you must jiggle the Analog Stick on your Xbox 360 controller about every ten minutes or your controller will shut off and the game will pause. If you have a subwoofer attached to your game system, you can use an object to balance your controller upside down on top of the subwoofer speaker (as long as your parents don't mind a little extra racing noise). The vibrations from the subwoofer speaker should be enough to keep the Analog Stick moving slightly and the controller won't turn off and pause the game. Even if you don't have a subwoofer, the Analog Stick is sensitive to any sort of movement, so be creative!

TIP: *Don't worry about tuning your car setups for your hired drivers—those setups are for you! If you need faster results in an endurance race and you can't upgrade your car components, hire a driver who demands more money. The best and most aggressive drivers might charge you for 90% to 100% of your winnings, but the trophies, unlocked cars, and Gamerscore Achievements are yours to keep!*

Be a Big Winner in the Proving Grounds Heavyweight Open

Many racers floor it all the way to Level 50 without ever finding a qualifying car for the Level 10 Heavyweight Open Series. The trick to qualifying isn't finding a fast car that weighs 3,850 lbs. (or 1,746 kg.)—you can also customize one of your existing race cars so it can qualify without falling behind at the starting line!

These weighty winners are some of the fastest you'll find:

+ Aston Martin V12 Vanquish
+ Audi RS 6
+ Bentley Continental GT
+ Cadillac CTS-V
+ Dodge Charger SRT-8 (for sale when you reach Level 18)
+ Ferrari 575M (with Forza Race Front Bumper, Rear Wing, and Rear Bumper installed)
+ Ferrari 612 Scaglietti
+ Mercedes CLK55 AMG Coupe

On other cars, add front bumpers, rear wings, rear bumpers, and wide heavy wheels to meet the qualifying weight for the Heavyweight Open. Pay attention to the speed ratings for your modified vehicles or you might find yourself quickly off the pace against rivals with monstrous horsepower!

Forza Motorsport 2 Xbox LIVE Gamerscore Achievements

Achievement	How to Earn It	Points
Flawless Lap	Finish a lap without a time penalty	5
Flawless Race	Finish a race without a time penalty	5
Natural	Win a race with all assists off	5
Hardcore	Win a race with all assists off and full difficulty on	5
Underdog	Win a race in a car with the lowest points in the race	5
Blowout	Win a race while leading the field by an entire track section	5
Crushing Victory	Win a race and lap a rival	5
Hard Charger	Win a race after starting in 8th place	5
Car Level 5	Earn car level 5 with a vehicle in Career mode	5
Level 1	Reach level 1 in Career mode	5
Level 10	Reach level 10 in Career mode	15
Level 20	Reach level 20 in Career mode	20
Level 30	Reach level 30 in Career mode	30
Level 40	Reach level 40 in Career mode	40
Level 50	Reach level 50 in Career mode	50
All Time Trials Set	Beat all target times in Time Trial mode	40
All Bronze Arcade	Earn a Bronze medal in every Arcade race	15
All Silver Arcade	Earn a Silver medal in every Arcade race	25

Achievement	How to Earn It	Points
All Gold Arcade	Earn a Gold medal in every Arcade race	35
All Gold (Proving Grounds)	Earn gold medals in every Proving Grounds Career mode race	20
All Gold (Manufacturer Club)	Earn gold medals in every Manufacturer Club Career mode race	20
All Gold (Amateur Cup)	Earn gold medals in every Amateur Cup Career mode race	25
All Gold (Rivalry Face-offs)	Earn gold medals in every Rivalry Face-offs Career mode race	30
All Gold (Semi-Pro)	Earn gold medals in every Semi-Pro Career mode race	40
All Gold (Factory-Spec)	Earn gold medals in every Factory-Spec Career mode race	40
All Gold (Regional Championship)	Earn gold medals in every Regional Championship Career mode race	50
All Gold (Professional Series)	Earn gold medals in every Professional Series Career mode race	60
All Gold (Endurance)	Earn gold medals in every Endurance Career mode race	70
All Gold All Race Types	Earn gold medals in every Career mode race	75
All Cars from France	Collect all car models from France	5
All Cars from Germany	Collect all car models from Germany	15
All Cars from Italy	Collect all car models from Italy	10
All Cars from Japan	Collect all car models from Japan	30
All Cars from Korea	Collect all car models from Korea	1
All Cars from Spain	Collect all car models from Spain	1
All Cars from Sweden	Collect all car models from Sweden	1

Achievement	How to Earn It	Points
All Cars from the United Kingdom	Collect all car models from the UK	5
All Cars from the United States	Collect all car models from US	25
1,000,000 Online Credits	Earn a million credits from Career races and tournament winnings	30
Car Broker	Buy or sell ten cars at the online Auction House	20
Secret Collector 1	Collect all production cars	30
Secret Collector 2	Collect all tuner cars	30
Secret Collector 3	Collect all race cars	30
Secret Collector 4	Collect all cars in the game	30

HARVEST MOON

NINTENDO WII VIRTUAL CONSOLE

How to Find All 20 Endings in the Game!

Harvest Moon on the Wii Virtual Console features over 20 different endings—but the trick is knowing how to find them all! Here are tips for finding the endings.

Remember: *If you qualify for more than one ending, the game will choose it for you. For example, if you ship more than 200 tomatoes and more than 200 potatoes, the game will pick one of those two endings, but you won't see both of them.*

Ending	Conditions	Final Scene
1	Earn a Happiness score of less than 100. Earn less than 1000 gold.	You'll hear your dog barking as you leave your farm. This is the worst ending possible in the game.
2	Own 7–12 cows	Your cows trot toward you as you ring the bell.
3	Own 1–6 cows	You brush and milk a cow as livestock wander around.
4	Own 1+ chickens	While collecting eggs in your coop you accidentally drop an egg.
5	Own 1+ cows. Earn a 192–255 Love Score.	Your cow gives you a Large milk, and then you take a nap.
6	Ship 200+ corn	You're in your field watering the growing corn.
7	Ship 200+ tomatoes	You put tomatoes in your horse's saddlebags before taking a break.
8	Ship 200+ potatoes	You see your dog barking at a potato plant and then he chases after a mole.
9	Ship 200+ turnips.	You give a turnip to a Harvest Sprite
10	Still a bachelor at the end of the game. Earn a 100+ Happiness score.	Your dog and horse love you.
11	Still a bachelor at the end of the game. Earn an 800+ Happiness score.	As you chop wood, the mountain animals give you a Power Berry.
12	Marry Maria	You and Maria visit town.
13	Marry Ann	You and Ann take her newest invention to the store.
14	Marry Nina	After seeing a frog, you take Nina on a picnic.

Ending	Conditions	Final Scene
15	Marry Ellen	Ellen rides up to take you on a picnic!
16	Marry Eve	You and Eve share each other's company.
17	Still a bachelor at the end of the game. The total Love Rate score for all brides-to-be are 1500+. Earn an 800+ Happiness score.	All the girls notice you walking by.
18	Marry early enough in the game to have one child.	You and your wife watch your child crawl.
19	Marry as early as possible in the game so you can have two children. You must keep your wife very happy throughout the game to do this.	Your family arrives while you are working in the field and hugs you.
20	Marry as early as possible in the game so you can have two children. Own 1+ cows. Own 1+ chickens. Collect 10 Power Berries. Earn a 900+ Happiness score. Earn 10,000 gold. Hug your dog every day for 100+ times in the game (everyone forgets this step).	A big gathering—the best ending in game!

HARVEST MOON DS: ISLAND OF HAPPINESS
NINTENDO DS

Extreme Likes and Dislikes

What you give to your neighbors can create lifelong friendships or burning rivalries. This table shows you the absolute favorite gift for every character on the island, as well as what they detest. It's fun to experiment and see the reactions of characters when they receive a gift they can't stand, but don't give bad things to the person you plan to marry or you might be making it up to them for several seasons!

Character	Favorite Gift	Dislikes	Birthday	Marriage?
Alisa	Ice cream	Ultimate curry	Winter 17	No
Charlie	Dry curry	Eggplant	Summer 30	No
Chen	Noodles	Boot	Spring 17	No
Cliff	Finest curry	Fish bones	Summer 6	No
Denny	Sashimi	Junk ore	Fall 26	Yes
Doctor Trent	Milk	French fries	Fall 19	No
Eliza	Donut	Wool	Summer 12	No
Elliot	Stir-fried veggies	Milk	Summer 21	Yes
Felicia	Gratin	Rice soup	Fall 9	No
Gannon	Tempura rice	Pink diamond	Spring 27	No
Harvest Goddess	Strawberry	Boot	Spring 8	No
Julia	Yogurt	Large fish	Spring 6	Yes
Karen	Pizza	Eli leaves	Fall 15	No
Lanna	Yam pudding	Fish bones	Fall 2	Yes
Mirabelle	Cheese	Weeds	Spring 11	No

Character	Favorite Gift	Dislikes	Birthday	Marriage?
Natalie	Fruit sandwich	Toadstool	Summer 28	Yes
Nathan	French toast	Pink diamond	Fall 4	No
Pierre	Finest curry	Toadstool	Spring 13	Yes
Popuri	Omelet rice	Grape punch	Summer 3	No

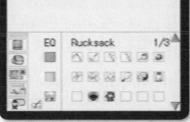

Character	Favorite Gift	Dislikes	Birthday	Marriage?
Regis	Pink diamond	Junk ore	Summer 17	No
Sabrina	Pink diamond	Rainbow curry	Winter 12	Yes
Shea	Large fish	Empty can	Winter 2	Yes
Taro	Eli leaves	Weeds	Winter 3	No
Vaughn	Porridge	Carrots	Spring 3	Yes
Wada	Grilled fish	Boot	Fall 20	No
Witch Princess	Rainbow curry	Peach	Winter 29	Yes

HARVEST MOON: MAGICAL MELODY
NINTENDO GAMECUBE, NINTENDO WII

Unlock Important Items!
Expand your farm and surroundings by completing these secret tasks:

Item	How to Earn It
Aging Pot	Earn five hearts from Saibara with gifts
Colored Vases	Mine and ship 10 good clays from your farm
Copper Fishing Rod	Find Ray at the Lake during daylight hours
Fertilizer	Ship at least 10 limestone from your farm
Level 3 Backpack	Earn three hearts from Martha and then bring her some yarn
Level 3 House	Earn a heart with Joe, Kurt, or Woody
Mixing Pot	Earn two-and-a-half hearts from Saibara with gifts
More Lots for Sale	Earn up to three hearts from the Mayor by giving him gifts
Pig	Build a Level 1 barn (and meet Gourmet at the Egg Festival)
Strawberry Seeds	Grow and ship at least 50 cabbages from your farm

Tip: *The pig helps you find truffles in the fall around the Mora trees. You can dig randomly without the pig to find these fall truffles—but it's more work and time out of your day!*

Gwen
When I come back again
please be kind to me!

Make Your Neighbors Return!

Hard economic times will force your neighbors to move off the island, but doing these tasks will bring them back to your village:

Neighbor	Task
Basil	Ship any herbs, flowers or Pontata Roots until he returns
Carl and Katie	Ship eggs and milk until they return
Dan	Ship 10 Very Berries
Dia and Gina	Ship herbs and Pontata Roots until they return
Eve	Ship grapes until she returns
Gwen	Ship 10 fish and 20 crops of any type
Ray	Ship fish of any type until he returns
Ron	Ship 10 fruits of any kind.

Give the Perfect Gifts Every Time!

You can quickly win friends and possibly a hand in marriage by giving the correct gifts to your neighbors in Harvest Moon: Magical Melody. Giving the wrong gifts will make your neighbors dislike you, so focus on giving these items instead:

Neighbor	Gift
Ann	Corn, Good eggs
Alex	Herbs, Fertilized turnips, Vegetable juice
Basil	Herbs, Herb tea, Tomato juice, Fertilized strawberries
Blue	Cheese, Eggs, Eggplants

Neighbor	Gift
Bob	Boiled eggs, Eggplants, Special eggs
Carl	Herb tea, Special milk
Dan	Sodas, Strawberries, Very berry jam
Dia	Blueberries and Blueberry jam, Moondrop flowers, Strawberries
Doug	Corn, Fertilized carrots, Fertilized green peppers
Duke	Boiled eggs, Grapes, Grape sodas, Special eggs
Ellen	Cocoa, Special eggs, Fertilized breadfruits
Eve	Apples, Fertilized strawberries, Strawberries, Wine
Gina	Blueberries, Eggs of all types, Shiny wool
Gourmet	Truffles and Truffle sautes
Gwen	Blueberries, Fertilized carrots, Shiny wool, Very berry jam
Hank	Apple Sodas, Fertilized turnips, Grape sodas
Henry	Apples, Fertilized carrots, Grapes
Jamie	Blueberry jam, Special milk, Strawberry jam, Very berry jam
Joe	Corn, most fish, Special eggs
Katie	Diamond rings, Special eggs, Very berries, Yams
Kurt	Herb tea, Gold, Wood
Liz	Eggplants, Purple balms, Yams
Louis	Moonstones, Special eggs
Lyla	Fertilized pumpkins, Pink balm, Pink cat flowers, Pumpkin puddings
Maria	Stewed potatoes, Stewed yams, Tomato soup
Martha	Cocoa, Fertilized breadfruits, Yarn
Mayor	Ores, most foods, both cooked and uncooked
Meryl	Boiled eggs, Fertilized tomatoes, Puddings, Special eggs
Michael	Copper ores, Fertilized onions, Fertilized potatoes, Special milk
Nami	Fertilized tomatoes, Special cheese, Tomato juice

Neighbor	Gift
Nina	Pink balm, Orange juice, Strawberries
Ray	Boiled eggs, Fertilized onions, Moonstones, most fish, Special eggs
Ronald	Grapes, Sodas
Saibara	Good clays, Pickled turnips, Sashimi
Tai	Fertilized eggplant, Fertilized spinach, Special milk, Rare ores
Terry	Fertilized cabbage, Fish, Good eggs, Mushrooms
Theodore	Fertilized potatoes, Stewed potatoes, Stewed yams
Tim	Boiled eggs, Chestnuts, Copper ores, Special eggs
Woody	Boiled eggs, Pickled turnips

HARVEST MOON: TREE OF TRANQUILITY
NINTENDO WII

Plant Your Orchards with a Plan!

Plenty of farmers plant apple trees, but if you stick to this traditional plan, you'll only profit from your mature trees in the fall. An easy way to spread out your profits is to plan your plots and sow seeds that deliver different types of produce throughout the year:

Tree or plant	Harvest in the
Cherry	Spring
Grape	Summer
Orange	Summer

Tree or plant	Harvest in the
Apple	Fall
Chestnut	Fall

Plant a few cherry trees for spring harvests, and then move along to picking grapes and oranges in the summer. Switch to apples and chestnuts in the fall. You must clear a 3 x 3 square area before planting a sapling, and any nearby rocks, weeds, or stumps will block the growing tree roots. Each young tree requires an entire year to mature, so plan your orchards far in advance!

What Can I Do When My Prize Cow Stops Producing Milk?

Cows eventually stop producing milk unless they give birth to a calf. Most cows produce milk for three or four seasons before you must buy a Miracle Potion for them. Because you can't milk a pregnant cow, you'll have an unproductive cow in your barn for at least a season.

Experienced Harvest Moon farmers rotate their pregnant cow schedules, so they always have some pregnant cows and some cows that produce milk (and money!) for their farm. For example, if you own four cows, use the Miracle Potion on one cow while the other three produce milk through the rest of the season. After a calf is born, use the potion on a different cow. This way, you never run out of fresh milk and income from your herd.

LEGO BATMAN: THE VIDEO GAME

XBOX 360, PLAYSTATION 2, PLAYSTATION 3, NINTENDO WII

Which Levels Still Have Missing Civilians?

Look for the frowning LEGO heads at the stage map screen. If you see a frown, there are still hostages or civilians who need help there. A smiling face means that you saved all the Gotham citizens in that area!

Levels with civilians include:	
Episode 1, Chapter 1	You Can Bank on Batman
Episode 1, Chapter 2	An Icy Reception
Episode 1, Chapter 4	A Poisonous Appointment
Episode 1, Chapter 5	Face Off
Episode 2, Chapter 1	There She Goes Again
Episode 2, Chapter 3	Under the City
Episode 2, Chapter 4	Zoo's Company
Episode 2, Chapter 5	Penguin's Lair
Episode 3, Chapter 1	Joker's Home Turf
Episode 3, Chapter 2	Little Fun at the Big Top

Levels with civilians include:

Episode 3, Chapter 4	In the Dark Night
Episode 3, Chapter 5	To the Top of the Tower
Episode 4, Chapter 1	The Riddler Makes a Withdrawal
Episode 4, Chapter 2	On the Rocks
Episode 4, Chapter 3	Green Fingers
Episode 4, Chapter 4	An Enterprising Theft
Episode 4, Chapter 5	Breaking Blocks
Episode 5, Chapter 1	Rockin' the Docks
Episode 5, Chapter 2	Stealing the Show
Episode 5, Chapter 4	A Daring Rescue
Episode 5, Chapter 5	Arctic World
Episode 6, Chapter 1	A Surprise for the Commissioner
Episode 6, Chapter 3	The Joker's Masterpiece
Episode 6, Chapter 4	The Lure of the Night
Episode 6, Chapter 5	Dying of Laughter

Tip: *Of all the civilian rescues, A Daring Rescue tends to be the one that stumps most caped crusaders. Go to the room with the red, green, and yellow pipes and use the Joker's Buzzer to start the generator and open a small metal gate. Enter the gate and go across the bridge to save the hostage!*

A Bright Idea

How many times have you taken a tumble off a ledge in the Bat Cave? Gotham is a dark place. If you play more than a stage, you've probably bumbled around in the dark or missed some important clues. Here's a simple trick to spot hidden surprises—turn up the brightness on your television. (If your parents don't like you adjusting the television settings, try playing the game with the room lights turned off—just watch your step when you get up to take a break!)

LEGO Batman: The Video Game Xbox LIVE Gamerscore Achievements

Achievement	How to Earn It	Points
Hero	Complete the first episode of the Hero campaign	25
Super Hero	Complete the second episode of the Hero campaign	25
Crusader	Complete the third episode of the Hero campaign	25
Villain	Complete the first episode of the Villain campaign	25
Super-Villain	Complete the second episode of the Villain campaign	25
Crime Lord	Complete the third episode of the Villain campaign	25
Sidekick	Complete a level with a second player (start in Batcave or Asylum)	15
Memorabilia	Collect all ten pieces of memorabilia in each level of the Villain and Hero campaigns	35
League of Assassins	Unlock all villains in the game	30
Justice League	Unlock all heroes in the game	30
It's the Car, Right?	Unlock all 22 vehicles in both Villain and Hero campaigns	30
1007 Mountain Drive	Complete the Wayne Manor bonus level (collect a million studs)	30
Unbreakable	Complete a level without being defeated and without extras enabled	30
0000001 00000011	Build the huge LEGO robot	20
The City is Safe... for now	Earn 100% in the game	50
Cobblepot School of Driving	Destroy all the cars in the robot level	20

Achievement	How to Earn It	Points
Vigilante	Rescue 25 civilians	25
Be a Hero	Be a Super Hero (full LEGO stud bars) for all levels in the Villain and Hero campaigns	40
Super Builder	Build 50 LEGO build-its	20
Nice Outfit!	Collect all suits	20
Dressed to Impress	Collect all 15 suit upgrades	20
The Richest Man in Gotham	Collect 4,000,000,000 (that's four billion) LEGO studs and max out your LEGO counter	40
The Most Dangerous Man on Earth	Use Batman to defeat Joker, Two-Face, Riddler, and Catwoman	20
Heads I Win, Tails You Lose	Defeat ten police officers and ten goons as Two-Face	20
Who Needs Curiosity?	Defeat Catwoman nine times (easiest when paired with Catwoman)	20
Shot to the Goon	Defeat eight goons in eight seconds	20
Throwing Up	Use superstrength (with Bane, Man-Bat, Clayface, or Killer Croc) to throw police officers 50 times	20
Atomic Backbreaker	Do the Backbreaker move on Batman while playing as Bane	20
Oh, I Got a Live One Here!	Shock thirty enemies with Joker's Hand Buzzer	10
Kill-a Moth	Defeat Killer Moth	20
Smash Gordon	Use Harley Quinn's Hammer to defeat Commissioner Gordon	20
Start of Something Wonderful	Shock the Joker with the Joker in Free Play	15
Boy Wonder	Use Robin to complete 20 back flips in a row	10

Achievement	How to Earn It	Points
Thanks a Million	Complete the Arkham Bonus Room	30
Is it a Bird? Is it a Plane?	Glide for 9 seconds with the Glide Suit	10
Gentleman, Start Your Screaming	Use a vehicle to knock over five enemies at once	15
Natural Habitat	Destroy the 21 street lights in Episode 1, Chapter 1	10
Make it Snappy	Build the Croc ride on	20
The Destroyer of Worlds	Use Bat Bombs to destroy a dozen objects in one blast	15
There and Back	Destroy ten objects in a single Batarang throw	10
Kiss from a Rose	Consume 15 foes using the Venus ride on or eat your partner 15 times	15
Ice to See You	Freeze 50 enemies using Mr. Freeze	15
Say Hello to My Little Friends	Defeat 20 police officers by using penguin bombers	15
Scare Tactics	Scare five enemies using Scarecrow	10
Down the Rabbit Hole	Walk five enemies off a ledge using Mad Hatter's mind control	20
Eat Floor... High Fiber	Slam 20 goons into the floor using Batman	15

LEGO INDIANA JONES: THE ORIGINAL ADVENTURES

XBOX 360, PLAYSTATION 2, PLAYSTATION 3, NINTENDO WII

Special Delivery!

After you complete a level in Story mode, revisit it in Free Play and look for the red parcels. Red parcels contain special extras that you can buy in the Barnett College mail room (the room directly across the main hall from the classroom). There's a trick to getting most red parcels and you must take along a character or two with special abilities to find these rare objects.

Here are the levels and skills essential for unlocking all the red parcels in the game:

Level	You Need a Character with	Parcel Contents (Stud Cost)
The Lost Temple	Thuggee Chant ability	Fast Fix (30,000)
Into the Mountains	Enemy Disguise ability	Super Slap (25,000)
City of Danger	Academic ability	Treasure x2 (1,000,000)
The Well of Souls	No special ability	Fast Dig (50,000)

Level	You Need a Character with	Parcel Contents (Stud Cost)
Pursuing the Ark	Explosives ability	Fast Build (40,000)
Opening the Ark	Academic ability	Artifact Detector (250,000)
Shanghai Showdown	Explosives ability	Treasure x4 (2,000,000)
Pankot Secrets	Thuggee Chant ability	Poo Treasure (70,000)
The Temple of Kali	Repair and Academic abilities	Super Scream (80,000)
Free the Slaves	Explosives ability	Character Treasure (100,000)
Escape the Mines	Academic ability	Treasure x6 (3,000,000)
Battle on the Bridge	Explosives ability	Regenerate Hearts (150,000)
The Hunt for Sir Richard	Tiny Size ability	Parcel Detector (125,000)
Castle Rescue	Thuggee Chant and Explosives abilities	Disarm Enemies (100,000)
Motorcycle Escape	Super Jump ability	Treasure x8 (4,000,000)
Trouble in the Sky	No special ability	Treasure Magnet (100,000)
Desert Ambush	Super Jump ability	Treasure x10 (5,000,000)
Temple of the Grail	Explosives ability	Invincibility (1,000,000)

After you find a parcel, look for a gray and red mailbox. If you can't find a mailbox, look for a stack of unassembled LEGO blocks—some mailboxes must be built before the parcels can be delivered!

Purple Studs Rule!

Purple studs are worth 10,000 LEGO studs, so if you see a purple stud, it's worth the time it takes to puzzle through the difficult maneuvers it takes to grab it.

LEGO Indiana Jones: The Original Adventures Xbox LIVE Gamerscore Achievements

Achievement	How to Earn It	Points
This... this is history...	Collect all artifacts in the game	40
Your mail is on your desk	Post all parcels	40
Fortune and glory, kid	Earn a 100% completion rate	100
You chose...wisely	Unlock all of the characters in the game	30
You will become a true believer	Use a Thuggee Statue 20 times	20
Bad dates!	Give 20 bananas to monkeys	20
What a cautious fellow I am	Destroy 50 objects with explosives or the bazooka	20
You call this archaeology?	Use a scholar's academic ability 50 times	20
The best digger in Cairo	Use the excavation ability to uncover 50 pieces of buried treasure	20

Treasure Magnet

Achievement	How to Earn It	Points
Trouble with her is the noise	Destroy 50 objects or defeat 50 characters with the Scream and Super Scream abilities	20
Start the engines, Jock!	Repair items at least 50 times with a mechanically skilled character	20
How we say goodbye in Germany	Infiltrate 50 restricted enemy locations	20
There is nothing to fear here	Complete "The Lost Temple" in Story mode	10
It's important Marion, trust me	Complete "Into the Mountains" in Story mode	10
Belloq's staff is too long	Complete "City of Danger" in Story mode	10
Why did it have to be snakes?	Complete "The Well of Souls" in Story mode	10

Achievement	How to Earn It	Points
I'm making this up as I go along	Complete "Pursuing the Ark" in Story mode	10
Keep your eyes shut!	Complete "Opening the Ark" in Story mode	10
Short Round, step on it!	Complete "Shanghai Showdown" in Story mode	10
I had bugs for lunch!	Complete "Pankot Secrets" in Story mode	10
Kali Ma will rule the world!	Complete "Kali's Temple" in Story mode	10
Quit fooling around	Complete "Free the Slaves" in Story mode	10
Take the left tunnel!	Complete "Escape the Mines" in Story mode	10
Prepare to meet Kali!	Complete "Battle of the Bridge" in Story mode	10
X marks the spot!	Complete "The Hunt for Sir Richard" in Story mode	10
DON'T call me Junior!	Complete "Castle Rescue" in Story mode	10
We're not going in the boat?	Complete "Motorcycle Escape" in Story mode	10
No ticket	Complete "Trouble in the Sky" in Story mode	10
They're well out of range, Dad	Complete "Desert Ambush" in Story mode	10
He chose...poorly	Complete "Temple of the Grail" in Story mode	10
I hate these guys	Defeat 200 foes	20
It's not the years, honey...	Complete a level in Story or Free Play mode without being defeated	40
How dare you kiss me!	Use Indy's whip to catch and kiss Mario, Willie, and Elsa (easiest in two-player mode)	15

Achievement	How to Earn It	Points
Oh, it breaks the heart	Break 15 bottles over the heads of foes in Marion's bar	15
That belongs in a museum! (Secret)	Complete "Young Indy" in Story mode	10
Nice try, Lao Che! (Secret)	Use Indy to defeat Lao Che (easiest in two-player Free Play mode)	20
Goodbye, Dr. Jones (Secret)	Use Lao Che to defeat Indy (easiest in two-player Free Play mode)	20
I step on fortune cookie! (Secret)	Defeat 50 creepy crawlies (red bugs)	20
He no nuts. He's crazy! (Secret)	Break 250 LEGO objects	20
Hey! You call him Dr. Jones! (Secret)	Create a custom character at the art studio across the Barnett College courtyard	20
That's for blasphemy! (Secret)	Use Jones Sr. to defeat Indy	20
Show a little backbone, will ya? (Secret)	Defeat 100 snakes	20
Blow it up! (Secret)	Defeat five enemies with a single explosive (easiest in "Escape the Mines" and "Pankot Secrets" in Free Play mode)	40
I cant' believe what you did (Secret)	Disarm 100 enemies using your whip	20
Throw me the idol (Secret)	Use the Whip to grab items at least 150 times in the game	20
We go for a ride (Secret)	Use the Whip Swing move at least 250 times in the game	20
Got lost in his own museum (Secret)	Unlock the Secret Area inside the Barnett College Museum	30

A
B
C
D
E
F
G
H
I
J
K
L
M
N
O
P
Q
R
S
T
U
V
W
X
Y
Z

Achievement	How to Earn It	Points
Where Forrestal cashed in (Secret)	Collect a million LEGO studs in the Ancient City Level	30
A source of unspeakable power (Secret)	Build at least 250 LEGO structures	20
You cheat very big! (Secret)	Unlock all Extras	30

LEGO STAR WARS: THE COMPLETE SAGA

XBOX 360, PLAYSTATION 2, PLAYSTATION 3, NINTENDO WII

Grappling Hook or Double Jump?

The arms that you wield in LEGO Star Wars: The Complete Saga will determine how you get around to places throughout the game levels. If you choose a character with a blaster, you won't be able to use a double jump, but you can throw a grappling hook. If you choose a character with a Lightsaber instead of a blaster, you can use the double jump to reach high spaces.

May Dr. Jones be with You

To unlock Indiana Jones, go through the Bonus Room door in the Cantina and look for the door with the movie projector above

it. Go inside and watch the preview for the LEGO Indiana Jones game—or press the B Button to exit the room. When you return to the Bonus Room, you'll receive a message that Indiana Jones is unlocked. You can buy Indiana Jones at the Cantina counter.

LEGO Star Wars: The Complete Saga Xbox LIVE Gamerscore Achievements

Achievement	How to Earn It	Points
The Phantom Menace	Finish Episode I in Story mode	20
Attack of the Clones	Finish Episode II in Story mode	20
Revenge of the Sith	Finish Episode III in Story mode	20
A New Hope	Finish Episode IV in Story mode	20
The Empire Strikes Back	Finish Episode V in Story mode	20
Return of the Jedi	Finish Episode VI in Story mode	20
Collector	Unlock all characters in the game	60
Secret Master	Collect all Red Bricks in the game	60
Going for Gold	Collect all Gold Bricks in the game	60
Mini Mayhem	Collect all Mini-Kits in the game	60
100%	Reach 100% complete (check your progress in the Cantina)	100
Lightsaber Master	Perform 20 unblockable combos	20
Lightsaber Defender	Perform 200 perfect lightsaber deflections	20
Dodger	Perform 200 blaster dodges	20
Stormtrooper Slayer	Defeat 300 stormtroopers	20
Droid Slayer	Defeat 300 droids	20
Fighter Ace	Defeat 50 TIE fighters	20
Yee Haw	Ride all mounts and ride-ons in the game	20
Cash In	Sell your Landspeeder to the Jawas	20
Crowd Pleaser	Break Jar-Jar Binks 20 times	20
Slam Dunk	Destroy five targets in one attack (the Jedi Super Slam)	20
Harmless?	Disable five Droidikas using R2D2	20
Fire in the Hole	Defeat ten targets with one thermal detonator	20

Achievement	How to Earn It	Points
Let the Wookie Win	Pull 25 arms off of different LEGO characters	20
Disco King	Set off all three Discos	20
Use the Force Luke	Complete Death Star Trench Run without firing a shot	20
Bar Room Brawl	Start a fight in the Cantina that results in 50 casualties	20
LEGO Build-Master	Create at least 100 build-its in the game	20
Gopher	Max out your Stud Counter	20
Cloud Cover	Finish Cloud City while still wearing a helmet	20
Follower of Fashion	Wear all hats in the game	20
Undecided	Defeat Anakin while using Darth Vader	10
Love is...	Defeat Jango Fett while using Boba Fett	10
Unfaithful	Defeat the Emperor while using Darth Maul	10
Did I Break Your Concentration?	Defeat the Emperor while using Mace Windu	10
Nobody Expects...	Defeat the Emperor while using Kit Fisto	10
Hands Off!	Defeat Anakin while using Dooku	10
Who Needs Obi-Wan?	Defeat Darth Maul while using Qui-Gon	10
Strike Me Down	Defeat Darth Vader while using Obi-Wan	10
Arcade Master	Earn 100 points in Arcade Mode	20
Online Player	Complete an entire game level online	20
Shoot First	Choose Han and Greedo in two-player Arcade and then let Han take the first shot	20

A
B
C
D
E
F
G
H
I
J
K
L
M
N
O
P
Q
R
S
T
U
V
W
X
Y
Z

Indiana Jones is now available to buy in the op.

LEGO STAR WARS II: THE ORIGINAL TRILOGY

XBOX 360, PLAYSTATION 2, PLAYSTATION 3, NINTENDO WII

Luke Skywalker and Princess Leia Unlocks!

While you can start the game with Princess Leia as a playable character, there are several special versions you can unlock as you progress through the game. Finish these chapters to unlock additional versions of these two favorite Star Wars heroes:

To Unlock Character	Finish This
Princess Leia (Bespin)	Chapter 6, Episode V
Luke Skywalker (Bespin)	Chapter 5, Episode V
Princess Leia (Boushh)	Chapter 1, Episode VI
Luke Skywalker (Dagobah)	Chapter 4, Episode V
Princess Leia (Endor)	Chapter 3, Episode VI
Luke Skywalker (Endor)	Chapter 3, Episode VI
Princess Leia (Hoth)	Chapter 2 in Episode V
Luke Skywalker (Hoth)	Chapter 1, Episode V and buy at the Cantina for 14,000 LEGO studs
Luke Skywalker (Jedi)	Chapter 1, Episode IV
Luke Skywalker (Pilot)	Chapter 4, Episode V
Princess Leia (Prisoner)	Chapter 6, Episode V and buy at the Cantina for 22,000 LEGO studs
Princess Leia (Slave)	Chapter 2, Episode VI
Luke Skywalker (Stormtrooper)	Chapter 4, Episode IV

LEGO Star Wars II: The Original Trilogy Xbox LIVE Gamerscore Achievements

Achievement	How to Earn It	Points
Secret Plans level complete	Complete the Secret Plans level at the beginning of the game	20
Episode IV complete	Finish Episode IV	50
Episode V complete	Finish Episode V	50
Episode VI complete	Finish Episode VI	50
LEGO City complete	Finish the LEGO City level	50
Bounty Hunter Missions complete	Finish all ten bounty hunter missions	40
Game 20% complete	Score 20% at the save display in the Cantina	20
Game 40% complete	Score 40% at the save display in the Cantina	40

Achievement	How to Earn It	Points
Game 60% complete	Score 60% at the save display in the Cantina	60
Game 80% complete	Score 80% at the save display in the Cantina	80
Game 100% complete	Score 100% at the save display in the Cantina	180
Secret Plans undefeated	Finish Secret Plans without extras or being defeated	20
Jundland Wastes undefeated	Finish Jundland Wastes without extras or being defeated	20
Mos Eisley undefeated	Finish Mos Eisley without extras or being defeated	20
Rescue the Princess undefeated	Finish Rescue the Princess without extras or being defeated	20
Death Star Escape undefeated	Finish Death Star Escape without extras or being defeated	20
Rebel Attack undefeated	Finish Rebel Attack without extras or being defeated	20
Hoth Battle undefeated	Finish Hoth Battle without extras or being defeated	20
Echo Base undefeated	Finish Echo Base without extras or being defeated	20
Falcon Flight undefeated	Finish Falcon Flight without extras or being defeated	20
Dagobah undefeated	Finish Dagobah without extras or being defeated	20
Cloud City Trap undefeated	Finish Cloud City Trap without extras or being defeated	20
Bespin undefeated	Finish Bespin without extras or being defeated	20
Jabba's Palace undefeated	Finish Jabba's Palace without extras or being defeated	20
Carkoon undefeated	Finish Carkoon without extras or being defeated	20

Achievement	How to Earn It	Points
Speeder Showdown undefeated	Finish Speeder Showdown without extras or being defeated	20
Endor undefeated	Finish Endor without extras or being defeated	20
Jedi Destiny undefeated	Finish Jedi Destiny without extras or being defeated	20
Death Star II undefeated	Finish Death Star II without extras or being defeated	20

LITTLEBIGPLANET FOR THE PLAYSTATION 3
PLAYSTATION 3

Where's the Tail Decoration for the Wooden Steed in the Garden's Get-a Grip-Level?

In the Tutorial section of LittleBigPlanet (LBP), figuring out how to use the Popit Menu can be a little tricky. When you reach the Wooden Steed in Get a Grip, you'll see some bubble objects, including one that looks a bit like a canoe paddle. When you pick up the item, the woman will tell you to put a sticker on the Wooden Steed. Here's how to find your Steed tail:

+ Press Square to Open your Popit Menu.
+ Choose Stickers and Decorations on the Popit menu and then press X.
+ On the Popit Menu, press the R1 Button

to scroll right to Decorations.

+ Highlight the tail (it's the object below Switch Triggers) and press X.
+ Now put the tail on the Wooden Steed and you're ready to roll!

Ace Awards

If you can complete an LBP level without being defeated, you'll earn a special gift for acing the level. Here's the list of levels and the prizes for making it through intact:

Level	Prize
The Gardens—First Steps	Pirate Hook and Pirate Eye Patch
The Gardens—Get a Grip	Pirate Pants and Pirate Waistcoat
The Gardens—Skate to Victory	Pirate Hat
The Savannah—Swinging Safari	Ringmaster Jacket
The Savannah—Burning Forest	Mustache
The Savannah—Meerkat Kingdom	Monocle and Top Hat
The Wedding—The Wedding Reception	Wooden Sword
The Wedding—The Darkness	Roman Armor
The Wedding—Skulldozer	Roman Helmet

Level	Prize
The Canyons—Boom Town	Leather Gloves and Cowboy Boots
The Canyons—The Mines	Bandana and Jeans with Belt
The Canyons—Serpent Shrine	Cowboy Hat
The Metropolis—Lowrider	Dinosaur Tail
The Metropolis—Subway	Green Sock Puppet
The Metropolis—Construction Site	Dinosaur Mask
The Islands—Endurance Dojo	Japanese Festival Robe
The Islands—Sensei's Lost Castle	Googly Eye Glasses
The Islands—The Terrible Oni's Volcano	Japanese Festival Headband
The Temples—The Dancer's Court	Chicken Beak
The Temples—Elephant Temple	Chicken Tail
The Temples—Great Magician's Palace	Chicken Wings
The Wilderness—The Frozen Tundra	White Neon Eyes
The Wilderness—The Bunker	Neon Helmet
The Wilderness—The Collector's Lair	Neon Dress
The Wilderness—The Collector	Yellow Head

Bronze Trophy	How to Earn It
The Gardens	Complete all of the levels in The Gardens
The Savannah	Complete all of the levels in The Savannah
The Wedding	Complete all of the levels in The Wedding
The Canyons	Complete all of the levels in The Canyons
The Metropolis	Complete all of the levels in The Metropolis
The Islands	Complete all of the levels in The Islands

A B C D E F G H I J K L M N O P Q R S T U V W X Y Z

Bronze Trophy	How to Earn It
The Temples	Complete all of the levels in The Temples
Expert Creator	Complete all of the levels in the tutorial
Artist	Place a sticker in any level
Homemaker	Make at least ten stickers or decorations in your Pod
Fashion Sense	Make a costume for your sack boy from materials that include something for the head and body
Forager	Collect 25% of the prize bubbles in the story levels
Sticky Fingers	Collect 50% of the prize bubbles in the story levels
Treasure Hunter	Collect 75% of the prize bubbles in the story levels
2X Multiplier!	Earn a 2X multiplier
8X Multiplier!	Earn an 8X multiplier
Incredible Speed!	Travel at incredible speed
Incredible Height	Reach an incredible height
Friendly	Complete a level with at least one other player
Party Person	Complete an online level with three friends
Socialite	Complete an online level with three players who are not on your friends list
Top of the Class	Win a four-player game
Traveler	Complete a community level
FIRST!	Be among ten people to complete a community level
Opinionated	Tag a community level
Neighborhood	Heart five community levels
Networking	Heart three authors
Talkative	Post a comment on a community level
Creator	Build and save a level with the thermometer at least 30% full
Team Creator	Build and save a level with more than one player with the thermometer at least 30% full
Publisher	Publish a level

Bronze Trophy	How to Earn It
Look What I Made!	Your published level was played by five or more players

Silver Trophy	How to Earn It
Just Beginning	Finish all of the main path story levels
20X Multiplier!	Earn a 20X multiplier in the game
Hi Score	Collect a million points on all levels combined
Booty Master	Collect all the prize bubbles on the story levels
Dr. Frankenstein	Create a living creature with at least two eyes, two legs (or wheels), and a brain
Crowd Pleaser	A level you published was played by 50 or more people
Feel the Love	A level you published was hearted by ten or more people
Celebrity	You were hearted by five or more people as a player

Gold Trophy	How to Earn It
Play	Complete all of the Story levels without being defeated (except stages where you are automatically defeated to end the level)
Create	Your published level earned hearts by 50 people and you were hearted by 30 people
Share	Play 150 community levels, tag 50 community levels, and heart 10 community levels
100% Complete	Earn all LBP trophies in the game

Easy 1,000 Points!

Some of the first titles for Xbox 360, including Electronic Arts Madden NFL, offered an easy 1,000 Gamerscore Achievements. Here's how to do it:

Choose a highly rated team like the Indianapolis Colts and go up against one of the lower-rated teams, such as the New Orleans Saints. Extend the game time, and then settle in for a long simulated season. Even though the game tells you that you must complete 30 years of Franchise mode, you'll earn this accomplishment when the game ends after 28 seasons.

Madden NFL Gamerscore Achievements
Pass for 350 Yards
100 points

Pair the Indianapolis Colts against the New Orleans Saints. Remember to maximize your quarter time before starting a game.

Rush for 200 Yards
100 points

Use the same approach

you used for earning 350 passing yards in a game. Pair the Indianapolis Colts against the New Orleans Saints and remember to maximize your quarter time before starting a game.

Activate RS Card
10 points

Start a Franchise mode game and go to the season schedule. Click down on the Right Analog Stick and you'll open the RS Card Menu. That's it!

Win the Super Bowl
100 points

If you choose a good team to simulate in Franchise mode, there is a good chance that your team will make it to the Super Bowl several times.

Enter History Book
10 points

Simply open the History Book menu in Franchise Mode. You don't even have to play a game!

Complete 30 Years of
Franchise
400 points

It's not whether you win or lose in your 30 years of Franchise, but how

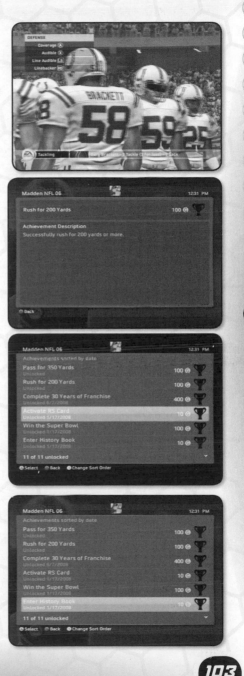

long you can simulate the game. While some hardcore gamers might want to play an entire season, you can select simulation for all 30 years and earn 400 Gamerscore Achievements in a few hours.

The following achievements don't require explanations and can be accomplished in a single game in Franchise mode. Most players use their favorite teams to unlock these Gamerscore Achievements, but if you have trouble earning four sacks, consider switching to a team with a tougher defense. New England is always a safe bet.

Achievement	Points
Win a Franchise Game	100
Four Sacks in One Game	100
Complete an Offline Game	30
Get a First Down	20
Score a Touchdown	30

MADDEN NFL FOOTBALL SERIES

XBOX, XBOX 360, PLAYSTATION 2, PLAYSTATION 3, NINTENDO WII, PSP, NINTENDO DS

Strength Matters in the Running Game

The most recent Madden titles factor in the ball carrier's strength when you press the Stiff-arm button, so be sure to consider the stiff-arm and trucking ratings. If you're going to play to win, especially against a team with an effective zone defense, you must know which running backs are the best in the game.

Running Backs

The highest-rated running backs in Madden NFL 09 are:

Running Back	Team
1. LaDainian Tomlinson	San Diego Chargers
2. Steven Jackson	St. Louis Rams
3. Brian Westbrook	Philadelphia Eagles
4. Adrian Peterson	Minnesota Vikings
5. Larry Johnson	Kansas City Chiefs
6. Fred Taylor	Jacksonville Jaguars
7. Marion Barber	Dallas Cowboys
8. Frank Gore	San Francisco 49ers
9. Willie Parker	Pittsburgh Steelers
10. Ronnie Brown	Miami Dolphins

Running Back Combinations

If you don't want to lose your star running back to injury, choose a team with a solid running game combination. The following teams have the highest-rated running back combinations in Madden NFL 09:

Team	Running Back Combinations
1. Jacksonville Jaguars	(Taylor and Jones-Drew)
2. Minnesota Vikings	(Peterson and Taylor)
3. Dallas Cowboys	(Barber and Jones)
4. Pittsburgh Steelers	(Parker and Mendenhall)
5. San Diego Chargers	(Tomlinson and Sproles)
6. New Orleans Saints	(McCalister and Bush)
7. Oakland Raiders	(Farges and McFadden)
8. Philadelphia Eagles	(Westbrook and Buckhalter)
9. Washington Redskins	(Portis and Betts)
10. Baltimore Ravens	(McGahee and Rice)

If your favorite team isn't listed among top-rated running backs but you still want to play using your favorite running plays, don't sweat it—just remember to press the Cover button in time to avoid a costly fumble and potential turnover.

Which Madden NFL Teams Rate Highest?

If you're having a tough time picking the best NFL team for a certain Madden season, make a game plan based on one of the following teams. Keep in mind that this list doesn't include All-Madden or hidden teams. If your opponent allows you to choose an All-Madden roster, that should be your first pick. Also remember that most Maddenoholics tend to think that their favorite team is the best team in the game, regardless of how the team is rated in defense, offense, and overall categories.

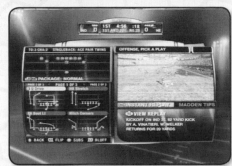

Season	Offense	Defense	Overall
Madden NFL 04	St. Louis	Miami/Tampa Bay	Miami/Tampa Bay
Madden NFL 05	New England/ Jacksonville	Indianapolis	New England
Madden NFL 06	Kansas City	New England	New England
Madden NFL 07	Indianapolis/ Seattle	Pittsburgh	Indianapolis
Madden NFL 08	San Diego	New England	New England
Madden NFL 09	Dallas	New England/ Baltimore	New England

Even if you don't have this chart handy, choosing the New England Patriots is usually a safe strategy.

Madden NFL 09 Xbox 360 Gamerscore Achievements

Achievement	How to Earn It	Points
Two TD Kickoff Returns in a Game	Return two-kickoffs for TDs in a game (non co-op)	75
Shut Out Rival in a Franchise	Shut out a Rival (hold to zero points) in a Franchise game (non co-op)	50
Kick a FG for over 50 Yards	Kick a field goal for over 50 yards in Franchise Mode (non co-op)	15
Complete a Game without an INT	Complete a game with at least five-minute quarters without an interception (non co-op)	30

Achievement	How to Earn It	Points
Six Rush TDs with the Dolphins	Earn six TDs rushing with the Miami Dolphins (non co-op)	50
Catch Ten Passes in a Game	Using one receiver, catch ten passes in a game (non co-op)	50
Complete a Game without Fumbling	Complete a game with at least five-minute quarters without a fumble (non co-op)	25
Two TD Punt Returns in a Game	Make two touchdown punt returns in a game (non co-op)	65
Intercept Six Passes in a Game	Intercept six passes in a game (non co-op)	50
Hold a Rival to under 300 Yards	Hold a rival team to under 300 yards of total offense in a game (non co-op)	50
Score 60 points in a Rival Game	Score 60 points in a Rival game (non co-op)	30
Score 40 Points in a Rival Game	Score 40 points in a Rival game (non co-op)	20
Record 12 Sacks in a Game	Make a dozen sacks in a game (non co-op)	50
Six Sacks with One Player in a Game	Make six sacks with one player in a game (non co-op)	50
80% Completion for a Game	Earn a 80% pass completion rate in a Franchise game with at least five-minute quarters (non co-op)	50
Seven Pass TDs with the Falcons	Throw seven passing TDs with the Falcons (non co-op)	50
550 Pass Yards with the Titans	Gain over 550 passing yards in a game using the Titans (non co-op)	50
300 Rush Yards with the Jets	Gain over 300 rushing yards in a game using the Jets	10
Hold a Rival to under 20 Points	Hold a Rival under 20 points in a game (set the quarters to one-minute lengths)	10

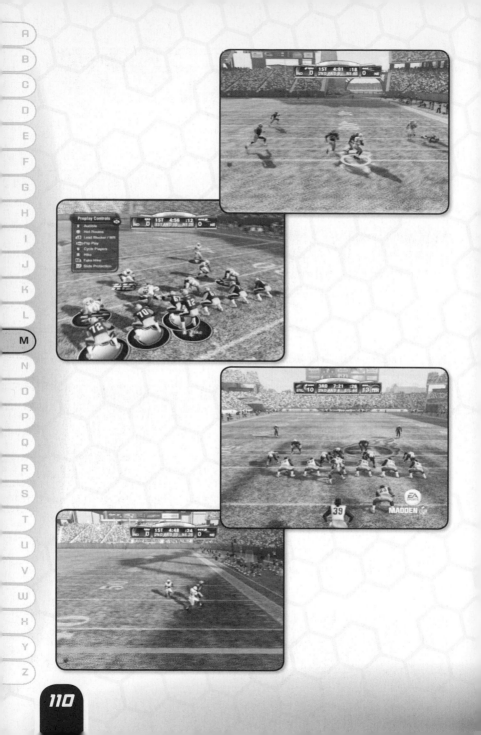

Achievement	How to Earn It	Points
Midway Monster	Create a legendary player from the past (create Bones Jackson for the Chicago Bears)	50
Can You Believe These Seats?!	Celebrate a touchdown in a wall hotspot	30
Steal Their Thunder	Steal an opposing player's touchdown celebration (press the B Button inside the end zone after a touchdown by the other team)	30
Slam Dunk All-Star	Dunk the ball over the goalpost after a touchdown (press the Y Button in the Blue Hot Spot area)	30
Shine in the Spotlight	Celebrate a touchdown by pressing the Y Button in the Blue Hot Spot area)	30
Now Here's a Guy...	Create a player in My Madden named John Madden	50

Living Rosters in Franchise Mode Concern?

Can the Living Rosters feature change your players in Franchise Mode? Although this was a concern in NBA 2K9, once you start a Franchise Mode season, your players and fantasy teams won't be modified by the Living Roster updates to Online and Play Now mode games.

Major League Baseball 2K9 Xbox LIVE Gamerscore Achievements

Achievement	How to Earn It	Points
Grand Poobah	Unlock all Achievements	150
Long Balls	Hit 25 home runs with your User Profile	5
Even More Long Balls	Hit 50 home runs with your User Profile	10
The Most Long Balls	Hit 100 home runs with your User Profile	20
Feel the Heat	Strike out 25 batters with your User Profile	5
That Guy's Not Throwing It Nice	Strike out 50 batters with your User Profile	10
There's a Hole in My Bat	Strike out 100 batters with your User Profile	20
Catch Me If You Can	Steal 25 bases with your User Profile	10

Achievement	How to Earn It	Points
Slippery When Wet	Steal 50 bases with your User Profile	20
Good Things Always Happen In 3s	Hit three home runs in a game	10
It's a Good Day to Be a Hitter	Hit four home runs in a game	20
Grab Some Pine	Strike out 12 batters in one game	10
Pining Away	Strike out 15 batters in one game	20
Unstoppable	Score 10 Runs in a Game	10
Has Anyone Seen the Fat Lady?	Score 15 runs in a game	20
Sticky Fingers	Steal four bases in one game	10
Cat Burglar	Steal six bases in one game	20
Flawless	Win a game without allowing any runs scored	20
Unhittable	Don't give up a hit in a game	20
It's Alive!	Create a Player	10
Man-Crush	Hit a Home Run with Tim Lincecum	10
Chicks Dig the Long Ball	Win the Classic Home Run Derby	10
I Could Have Been a Contender	Play a Ranked Online Exhibition Game	10
Two Turn Tables...	Create a 2K Beats playlist	10
Absolute Power	Hit 40 home runs in a season with one player (play at least 20 games without simulating)	20
May the Best Man...	Win 20 games in one season with a pitcher (play at least 20 games without simulating)	20
Centennial Man	Drive in 100 runs in a season with one player (play at least 20 games without simulating)	20

A
B
C
D
E
F
G
H
I
J
K
L
M
N
O
P
Q
R
S
T
U
V
W
X
Y
Z

Achievement	How to Earn It	Points
Show Stopper	Save 40 games in a season with one player (play at least 20 games without simulating)	20
Bicentennial Man	Strike out 200 batters in a season with one player (play at least 20 games without simulating)	20
There Can Be Only One	Win the World Series in Franchise mode (play at least 20 games without simulating)	20
If You Build It...	Create a card team	5
Spring Training	Try all four practice modes	5
King of the Hill	Top the Best of the Best ladder in Home Run Derby mode	5
Alone at the Top	Win the World Series in Postseason Mode (play the final game)	5
Team 2K	Defeat a Team 2K member or someone who has beat a Team 2K member in an online game	60
Hurlers	Unlock all the pitcher cards in the game	10
Crushers	Unlock all batter cards in the game	10
Teamwork	Unlock all nine cards for one team	5
Spread the Wealth	Unlock one card for each of the 30 MLB teams	5
A Man for All Seasons	Unlock 10 Classic Player Cards	10
One Hundo	Unlock 100 cards	10
Two Hundo	Unlock 200 cards	10
All the Tea...	Unlock all 320 cards	10
Hard Knocks (Secret)	Bean three batters in row	5

Hchievement	How to Earn It	Points
Vicious Cycle (Secret)	Hit through the cycle with a single player in a game	50
This Old Man Came Rolling Home (Secret)	Expect the Unexpected	50
Expect the Unexpected (Secret)	Drive in a run with a pitcher during a game	5
That's All Folks (Secret)	Hit a home run to win a game	50
Untouchable (Secret)	Use one pitcher to throw a no-hitter	50
Ya Can't Get Fooled Again (Secret)	Strike out the batter and throw out the runner on the same play	50

PlayStation 3 Trophies

Trophy	How to Earn It
Long Balls Bronze Trophy	Hit 25 home runs with your User Profile
Even More Long Balls Bronze Trophy	Hit 50 home runs with your User Profile
The Most Long Balls Bronze Trophy	Hit 100 home runs with your User Profile
Feel the Heat Bronze Trophy	Strike out 25 batters with your User Profile
That Guy's Not Throwing Nice Bronze Trophy	Strike out 50 batters with your User Profile
There's a Hole in My Bat Bronze Trophy	Strike out 100 batters with your User Profile
Catch Me if You Can Bronze Trophy	Steal 25 bases with your User Profile
Slippery When Wet Bronze Trophy	Steal 50 bases with your User Profile
Good Things Always Happen in 3s Bronze Trophy	Hit three home runs in a game
It's a Good Day to be a Hitter Bronze Trophy	Hit four home runs in a game

Trophy	How to Earn It
Grab Some Pine Bronze Trophy	Strike out 12 batters in one game
Pining Away Bronze Trophy	Strike out 15 batters in one game

MARIO KART DS
NINTENDO DS

Unlock New Courses!
Earn the following cups to unlock these courses:

Cup	Win
150cc Mirror	Gold trophies for all courses in the 150cc Retro Classes
Leaf Cup	Gold trophies for Shell Cup and Banana Cup
Lightning Cup	(Gold) for Leaf Cup
Special Cup	(Gold) on Star Cup
Star Cup	Gold trophies for Mushroom Cup and Flower Cup

Unlock Uther Items:

Daisy and Dry Bones	Gold trophies for all 50cc courses in the Nitro Grand Prix
More Karts	Gold trophies for all 100cc and 150cc courses in the Nitro Grand Prix
ROB64	Gold trophies for 150cc mirror Nitro Grand Prix
Waluigi	Gold trophies for all 100cc courses in the Nitro Grand Prix

Don't Worry about Squid Ink!

Experienced racers don't miss a turn when their top screens are covered with squid ink! Why? Because they use the map on the lower screen on their Nintendo DS. Even though the map screen won't show small obstacles, it will help you stay in the middle of the track until the squid ink rolls off your top screen.

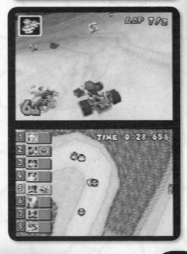

Starting Line Boost

All Mario Kart games feature a turbo-start secret—the trick is knowing when to hold your accelerator button. Watch the timer count down and press the 2 Button on your Wii Remote just as the number 2 on the timer begins to fade. If you've timed it right, you'll enjoy a small boost as the light goes green!

How Do I Unlock Expert Ghosts?

Unlock an Expert Staff Ghost by defeating the Regular Staff Ghost by at least seven seconds. You must unlock these faster Expert Staff Ghosts before you can unlock special characters like Baby Luigi and Funky Kong.

Racer Unlocks!

Here are all the unlockable racers in Mario Kart Wii. Unlike other Mario Kart games, you can unlock some of these characters two or three ways, but winning races is always the fastest—and sometimes the easiest! You need to meet only one goal to unlock a racer.

Kart Racer	Goal #1	Goal #2	Goal #3
Baby Daisy	Earn one star or higher in all Wii Cups	Race in 1,950 races	N/A
Baby Luigi	Open 8 Expert Staff Ghosts	Win 100 Wi-Fi Ghost races	Race in 3,150 races
Birdo	Finish 16 Time Trial courses	Win 250 Wi-Fi races	Race in 1,350 races
Bowser Junior	Earn 1 star or higher in all Retro Cups	Race in 3,450 races	N/A
Daisy	Finish 1st in the 150cc Special Cup	Race in 2,850 races	N/A
Diddy Kong	Finish 1st in the 50cc Lightning Cup	Race in 450 races	N/A
Dry Bones	Finish 1st in the 100cc Leaf Cup	Race in 1,050 races	N/A
Dry Bowser	Earn 1 star or more in all Wii Cups	Race in 4,350 races	N/A

Kart Racer	Goal #1	Goal #2	Goal #3
Funky Kong	Open 4 Expert Staff Ghosts	Win 25 Wi-Fi races	Race in 2,250 races
King Boo	Finish 1st in 50cc Star Cup	Race in 750 races	N/A
Rosalina	Earn 1 star or higher in all Mirror cups	Race in 4,950 races	Race in 50 races and have Super Mario Galaxy files saved to your Wii
Toadette	Finish all Time Trial courses	Win 1,000 Wi-Fi races	Race in 2,550 races

Mario Circuit

Striker Challenge Unlocks

Some gamers spend so much time in Domination, Wi-Fi, or Road to Striker Cup modes that they completely miss the benefits of playing Striker Challenge mode! Each time you complete a Striker Challenge, you earn a Player Card and unlock a special game or cheat feature. Here are the details:

Complete	Receive Player Card/Game Feature
Challenge 1	Mario/Classic Mode
Challenge 2	Luigi/Safe Megastrike
Challenge 3	Donkey Kong/Super Captains
Challenge 4	Peach/High Voltage
Challenge 5	Daisy/Devastating Hits
Challenge 6	Wario/No Power-Ups
Challenge 7	Waluigi/Secure Stadia
Challenge 8	Yoshi/Power Shortage
Challenge 9	Bowser/Field Tilt
Challenge 10	Petey Piranha/White Ball
Challenge 11	Bowser Jr./Sidekick Skill Shot
Challenge 12	Diddy Kong/Custom and Infinite Power-Ups

Striker Cup Winnings!

You can unlock new soccer venues by winning the following cups in Striker Cup mode:

Win Cup	Unlocks
Crystal	Crystal Cannon
Fire	The Lava Pit
Striker	Stormship Stadium

When you win a cup, you will also unlock these team captains:

Win Cup	Unlocks
Crystal	Diddy Kong
Fire	Bowser Jr.
Striker	Petey Piranha

You can also open these stadiums and locations if you win the Brick Wall and Golden Foot Awards during a tournament:

Win Cup	Unlocks
Crystal	The Dump
Fire	The Wastelands
Striker	Galactic Stadium

MARIO SUPER SLUGGERS
NINTENDO WII

Swing for the Stadium Unlocks!

You can unlock Stadiums by completing these tasks in Challenge mode:

Stadium	Condition for Unlock
Bowser Jr.'s Playroom	Defeat Bowser Jr. in his Playroom Stadium
Bowser's Castle	Defeat Bowser's team
Daisy's Cruiser	Buy the Cruiser Pass for 300 coins at Peach's Ice Garden after Peach joins the team
Luigi's Mansion	Buy the Flashlight for 300 coins at the Mario Stadium item shop

Unlock Hidden Mini Games!

While Mario Super Sluggers initially features three mini games, keep playing through Challenge mode and you'll unlock more mini games! Here are the conditions for adding games to the island:

Mini Game	Condition
Blooper Baserun	Open Daisy's Cruiser
Bomb-omb Derby	Defeat Bowser Jr. in Challenge mode
Castle Pinball	Open Bowser's Castle
Ghost K	Open Luigi's Mansion
Graffiti Runner	Open Bowser Jr.'s Playroom Stadium
Wall Ball	Defeat Bowser Jr. in Challenge mode

Mini games feature three difficulty levels: Mushroom, Flower, and Star. If you win all the mini games on Star level, you'll open a Mini Game Madness mode that offers a multiplayer contest where you randomly play five of the nine mini games in the game.

MLB: THE SHOW 09

PSP, PLAYSTATION 2, PLAYSTATION 3

Control Issues?

The pitching in MLB: The Show 09 is extremely realistic, especially in Road to the Show (RttS) mode. Gamers who are used to baseball games with arcade-like pitching find that aim-the-pitch-and-throw-hard strategies won't work. These pitching statistics can help your team win more RttS games:

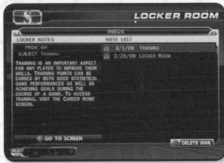

Stamina

Stamina points are a key factor if you're building a starting pitcher (SP), especially if you want to pitch beyond 80 pitches. Good closers and relief pitchers don't require as many stamina points.

Pitching Clutch

All types of pitchers require a solid Pitching Clutch score to help them deal with pressure in challenging situations. You want a clutch player who can handle loaded bases or a full pitch count in the late innings of a tied game.

H/9, HR/9, K/9, BB/9

Improve these attribute numbers to improve your score:

+ H/9 is your hits per inning. If you improve your H/9 score, the computer players are less likely to make contact with the ball, and when they do the ball won't carry as far.
+ A high HR/9 score means that your pitcher will give up fewer home runs.
+ K/9 is the number of strikeouts you'll earn in games.
+ A high BB/9 helps improve your control so you're less likely to give up walks. If you're looking for good control, raise your BB/9 attribute score through extra training.

Pitch Types, Control, Velocity, and Movement

With high attributes for Pitching Clutch and BB/9, you can build on the velocity, control, and movement in your pitches. Many new players dump points into the control attributes while ignoring other broad characteristics like BB/9 and Pitching Clutch. Remember: Any points spent on improving the control attributes of your fastball or curveball only work for that one pitch—but if you spend more points in BB/9 or Pitching Clutch, you improve the results for every pitch that you deal from the mound.

PS3 Game Trophies

Title	Trophy	How to Earn It
The Salami	Bronze	Hit a grand slam
Walk-off Win	Bronze	Win a game with a walk-off hit or a walk
Road to the Show Power Plays	Bronze	Hit two home runs in a RttS game on All-Star or a higher difficulty level

Title	Trophy	How to Earn It
Road to the Show In Control	Bronze	Strike out ten batters in a single RttS game on All-Star or a higher difficulty level
Make the Call	Bronze	Be called up to an MLB team
Road to the Show Streaker	Bronze	Earn a ten-game hitting streak in RttS mode without simulating a game
Stop Thief!	Bronze (Secret)	Steal three bases in one RttS game
It Happens to Everyone	Bronze (Secret)	Lose 100 games combined in all modes
Net Works	Bronze	Win five games online
It Takes Time: Hits	Bronze	Earn 1,000 hit combined in all game modes
It Takes Time: Strike Outs	Bronze	Strike out 500 batters combined in all game modes
It Takes Time: RBI	Bronze	Earn 1,500 RBIs combined in all game modes
It Takes Time: HR	Bronze	Hit 300 home runs combined in all game modes
Managerial	Bronze	Win a Manager Mode game in Season, Franchise, or Manager Mode.
Shut em' Out	Bronze	Pitch a shut out against the computer in All-Star or a higher difficulty level
Walk off in Style	Silver	Win a game with a walk-off home run
Don't Hit Me	Silver	Pitch a no-hitter against the computer in All-Star or a high difficulty level

Title	Trophy	How to Earn It
Streaker: Team	Silver	Earn a ten-game winning streak in Franchise or Season mode against the computer—but don't simulate any games!
Road to the Show Streaker: Batter	Silver	Earn a 20-game hitting streak during the regular season in RttS mode—but don't simulate any games!
Road to the Show Streaker: Pitcher	Silver	Earn a ten-game win streak during the regular season in RttS mode—and don't simulate any games
Road to the Show Added Value	Silver	Win an MLB award in RttS mode
Major Leaguer	Silver	Join an online league and complete at least 60% of the games
Road to the Show Streaker: Batter	Gold	Earn a 50-game game hitting streak during the regular season in RttS mode—but don't simulate any games!
Road to the Show Streaker: Pitcher	Gold	Earn a 15-game win streak during the regular season in RttS mode—and don't simulate any games
Road to the Show MVP	Gold	Win the MLB MVP award in RttS mode
Road to the Show The Cycle	Gold	Hit through the cycle with a RttS player
Road to the Show Personal Perfection	Gold	Pitch a perfect game with a RttS player on All-Star or higher difficulty settings
Online Legend	Gold	Win an online league while playing at least 60% of the games
100% Clear	Platinum	Unlock all of the trophies in the game

A
B
C
D
E
F
G
H
I
J
K
L
M
N
O
P
Q
R
S
T
U
V
W
X
Y
Z

MONSTERS VS. ALIENS
XBOX 360, PLAYSTATION 3

Unlock the Dreamworks Fan Exclusive Scoring Badge!

If you have a saved file from another recent Dreamworks game title (like Madagascar: Escape 2 Africa) on your Xbox 360 or PlayStation 3, you can access the Dreamworks Fan Exclusive Scoring Badge. This will add a Special Bonus to the end of your stage score! To unlock the badge, select "Special Features" at the Main menu.

Monsters vs. Aliens PlayStation 3 Trophies

Title	Trophy	How to Earn It
Is There a Way Out?	Bronze	Complete Chapter 1
San Francisco is Safe, Next!	Bronze	Complete Chapter 2
Could We Fight Something Bigger?	Bronze	Complete Chapter 3
What Alien Menace?	Bronze	Complete Chapter 4
Flying Fish	Bronze	Perform 50 Leap Attacks with The Missing Link
Stay Put and Watch	Bronze	Watch the game credits all the way to the end

(DR. COCKROACH) IT'S THE LIGHTS ON THE HELICOPTER - THEY'VE HYPNOTIZED INSECTOSAURUS!

Title	Trophy	How to Earn It
Casual Collector	Bronze	Collect 100,000 Monster DNA particles
Full Arsenal	Bronze	Buy all upgrades for every character (the green nodes in the lab)
Two is Better than One	Bronze	Buy all Co-op mode upgrades
Art Aficionado	Bronze	Buy all concept art
Shopping Frenzy	Bronze	Buy all surprises (the purple nodes in the lab)
That's a Blast	Bronze	In Co-op mode, use the Charge Blast for the first time
Strong Attraction	Bronze	In Co-op mode, use the Tractor Beam for the first time
Collateral Damage	Bronze	In Co-op mode, defeat 30 EyeScouts and helicopters in Ginormica's levels

Title	Trophy	How to Earn It
Air Support Master	Bronze	In Co-op mode, defeat 100 BHolders in The Missing Link's and B.O.B.'s levels
Maximum Attraction	Bronze	In Co-op mode, Tractor Beam 50 enemies in The Missing Link's and B.O.B.'s levels
Great Tackler	Bronze	Use Ginormica's Dash to defeat ten drones
Master Tackler	Bronze	Use Ginormica's Dash to defeat 25 drones
Get Out of the Way	Bronze	Use Ginormica's Chain Dash for the first time
Bring It On	Bronze	Defeat a Beam Bot without taking damage
Just Warming Up	Bronze	Use The Missing Link to defeat 50 enemies
Can't Get Enough!	Bronze	Use The Missing Link to defeat 100 enemies
Bull Rider	Bronze	Destroy 10 Turrets in Rodeo mode while climbing with The Missing Link
Cowboy Master	Bronze	Destroy 30 Turrets in Rodeo mode while climbing with The Missing Link
Strike with Attitude	Bronze	Use The Missing Link's Leap Attack for the first time
Expert Pitcher	Bronze	Use The Missing Link to throw 25 enemies
Pinball Fan	Bronze	Use the Bumpers for the first time
Around the World	Bronze	Use the Pole Vault for the first time
Glutton	Bronze	Use B.O.B. to swallow 20 enemies or objects

Title	Trophy	How to Earn It
Machine Gun Specialist	Bronze	Complete a B.O.B Turret sequence without being hurt
Safety First	Bronze	Activate B.O.B's Shield for the first time
Olympic Champion	Bronze	Earn any Medal in all Monster Challenges
My Thumb Hurts	Bronze	Earn 5,000,000 points
Not a Novice Anymore	Silver	Complete the game
Could I Be Any Better Than This?	Silver	Use The Missing Link to defeat 300 enemies
Gourmet	Silver	Use B.O.B. to swallow 50 enemies or objects
Never Say Enough	Gold	Collect 500,000 Monster DNA particles
Gold Olympic Champion	Gold	Earn a Gold Medal in all Monster Challenges
Be My Guest	Gold	Earn 10,000,000 points
Defying Gravity	Bronze (secret)	Jump at least 150 times with each monster
Team Spirit	Bronze (secret)	Complete Chapter 1 without failing more than 10 times
Team Victory	Bronze (secret)	Complete Chapter 2 without failing more than 10 times
Team Glory	Silver (secret)	Complete Chapter 3 without failing more than 10 times
Team Supremacy	Silver (secret)	Complete Chapter 4 without failing more than 10 times
Remember the Heroes	Gold (secret)	Complete the entire game without failing more than 10 times
Monsters vs. Aliens Champion	Platinum (secret)	Unlock all 45 trophies in the game

Monsters vs. Aliens Xbox LIVE Gamerscore Achievements

Achievement	How to Earn It	Points
Is There a Way Out?	Complete Chapter 1	20
San Francisco is Safe, Next!	Complete Chapter 2	25
Could We Fight Something Bigger?	Complete Chapter 3	30
What Alien Menace?	Complete Chapter 4	35
Flying Fish	Perform 50 Leap Attacks with The Missing Link	20
Stay Put and Watch	Watch the game credits all the way to the end	5
Casual Collector	Collect 100,000 Monster DNA particles	20

Achievement	How to Earn It	Points
Full Arsenal	Buy all upgrades for every character (the green nodes in the lab)	30
Two is Better than One	Buy all Co-op mode upgrades	15
Art Aficionado	Buy all concept art	30
Shopping Frenzy	Buy all surprises (the purple nodes in the lab)	15
That's a Blast	In Co-op mode, have your partner use the Charge Blast for the first time	10
Strong Attraction	In Co-op mode, have your partner use the Tractor Beam for the first time	10
Collateral Damage	In Co-op mode, have your partner defeat 30 EyeScouts and helicopters in Ginormica's levels	10
Air Support Master	In Co-op mode, have your partner defeat 100 BHolders in The Missing Link's and B.O.B.'s levels	20
Maximum Attraction	In Co-op mode, have your partner Tractor Beam 50 enemies in The Missing Link's and B.O.B.'s levels	10
Great Tackler	Use Ginormica's Dash to defeat ten drones	15
Master Tackler	Use Ginormica's Dash to defeat 25 drones	20
Get Out of the Way	Use Ginormica's Chain Dash for the first time	10
Bring It On	Defeat a Beam Bot without taking damage	10
Just Warming Up	Use The Missing Link to defeat enemies	50
Can't Get Enough!	Use The Missing Link to defeat 100 enemies	35

Achievement	How to Earn It	Points
Bull Rider	Destroy 10 Turrets in Rodeo mode while climbing with The Missing Link	10
Cowboy Master	Destroy 30 Turrets in Rodeo mode while climbing with The Missing Link	20
Strike with Attitude	Use The Missing Link's Leap Attack for the first time	10
Expert Pitcher	Use the Missing Link to throw 25 enemies	10
Pinball Fan	Use the Bumpers for the first time	10
Around the World	Use the Pole Vault for the first time	10
Glutton	Use B.O.B. to swallow 20 enemies or objects	15
Machine Gun Specialist	Complete a B.O.B Turret sequence without being hurt	20
Safety First	Activate B.O.B's Shield for the first time	10
Olympic Champion	Earn any medal in all Monster Challenges	10
My Thumb Hurts	Earn 5,000,000 points	20
Not a Novice Anymore	Complete the game	40
Could I Be Any Better Than This?	Use the Missing Link to defeat 300 enemies	35
Gourmet	Use B.O.B. to swallow 50 enemies or objects	30
Never Say Enough	Collect 500,000 Monster DNA particles	70
Gold Olympic Champion	Earn a Gold Medal in all Monster Challenges	30
Be My Guest	Earn 10,000,000 points	50

Achievement	How to Earn It	Points
Defying Gravity (Secret)	Jump at least 150 times with each monster	50
Team Spirit (Secret)	Complete Chapter 1 without failing more than 10 times	10
Team Victory (Secret)	Complete Chapter 2 without failing more than 10 times	10
Team Glory (Secret)	Complete Chapter 3 without failing more than 10 times	25
Team Supremacy (Secret)	Complete Chapter 4 without failing more than 10 times	35
Secret Achievement (Secret)	View all the credits and then keep playing	80

MOTOGP 06

XBOX 360

Faster Race Seedings in Career Mode

Earning all of the Career Seeding Achievements in MotoGP '06 will take hours, but you can speed up your rise to the top by reducing each race to a single lap. You must still race hard and fast, but these one-lap contests advance your career much faster than playing the game on default settings. The trick is knowing how to reduce race laps, because the game designers didn't make it an obvious option in Career Mode.

- ✦ At the Main Menu, choose Single Player, and then Racing Career.
- ✦ Choose Any Class and press the Y Button to access the Options Menu.
- ✦ At the Options menu, change the Laps setting from three laps to one lap.
- ✦ Now you're geared to roll through some fast seedings!

MotoGP 06 Xbox LIVE Gamerscore Achievements

Achievement	How to Earn It	Points
Seeded #1	Reach #1 on the seeding rank	75
Seeded #10	Reach #10 on the seeding rank	50
Seeded #25	Reach #25 on the seeding rank	30
Seeded #50	Reach #50 on the seeding rank	20
Seeded #75	Reach #75 on the seeding rank	15
Seeded #90	Reach #90 on the seeding rank	10

Achievement	How to Earn It	Points
GP – Legend	Win a Grand Prix season in Career mode on Legend difficulty	100
GP – Champion	Win a Grand Prix season in Career mode on Champion difficulty	60
GP – Professional	Win a Grand Prix season in Career mode on Professional difficulty	30
Challenge Master	Complete all Challenges in the game	60
Challenge Expert	Complete 50 Challenges in the game	30
Extreme Bike Collector	Buy all Extreme mode bikes in the game	50
Stunt Mode Rider	Complete a Stunt Mode game in multiplayer	10
Extreme 1200 – Legend	Win the Extreme 1200 season in Career mode on the Legend difficulty setting	75

Achievement	How to Earn It	Points
Extreme 1200 – Champion	Win the Extreme 1200 season in Career mode on the Champion difficulty setting	75
Extreme 1200 – Professional	Win the Extreme 1200 season in Career mode on the Professional difficulty setting	75
Extreme 1000 – Legend	Win the Extreme 1000 season in Career mode on the Legend difficulty setting	75
Extreme 600 – Legend	Win the Extreme 600 season in Career mode on the Legend difficulty setting	75
Extreme Mode Champion	Win the Championship in Extreme mode on any difficulty setting	10
Accredited	Win all rider credit awards	100
GP – Rookie	Win the Grand Prix season in Career mode on the Rookie difficulty setting	10

MYSIMS: KINGDOM

NINTENDO WII

Know Where to Cast to Find the Right Fish!

Fish	Location
Angler Fish	Trevor Island
Bass	Cowboy Junction
Batfish	Spookane
Betta	Candypalooza
Catfish	Renee's Nature Preserve
Crab	Cowboy Junction, Forest of the Elves, Rocket Reef
Electric Eel	All fishing locations
Goby	Candypalooza, Cowboy Junction, Forest of the Elves, Rocket Reef, Royal Academy, Spookane
Gold Arowana	Forest of the Elves
Jellyfish	Cowboy Junction, Renee's Nature Preserve
Koi	Forest of the Elves
Marlin	Forest of the Elves
Octopus	Royal Academy
Piranha	Cowboy Junction, Rocket Reef, Spookane
Plecostomous	Spookane
Puffer	Uncharted Isle
Robofish	Rocket Reef
Sea Turtle	Cutopia, Spookane, Trevor Island, Uncharted Isle
Sea Urchin	Forest of the Elves, Rocket Reef, Spookane
Seahorse	Royal Academy
Squid	Candypalooza
Stingray	Uncharted Isle
Sunfish	Cutopia
Tiny Shark	Forest of the Elves

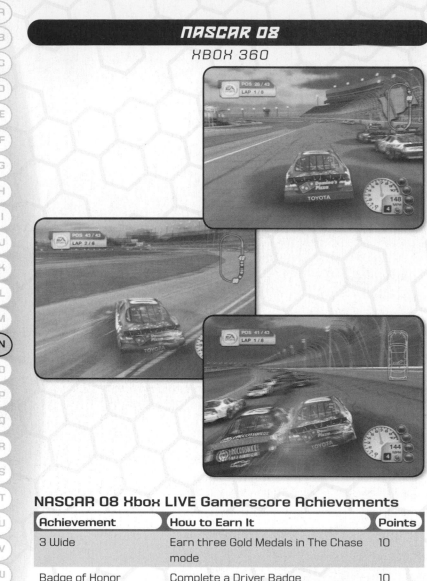

NASCAR 08 Xbox LIVE Gamerscore Achievements

Achievement	How to Earn It	Points
3 Wide	Earn three Gold Medals in The Chase mode	10
Badge of Honor	Complete a Driver Badge	10
We're Talkin' About Practice	Record a Lap in Toyota Test and Tune mode	10
Keep On Truckin'	Win a Craftsman Truck Series race	10

Achievement	How to Earn It	Points
Custom Car Creator	Complete a Custom Car for all racing series	10
Heavy Medal	Win a medal in The Chase mode	10
Play it Again, Sam	Save a Race Replay	10
Today or Tomorrow?	Win a NASCAR Car of Tomorrow race	10
Trade your Setup	Upload a Car Setup to EA Locker	10
National Hero	Win a NASCAR National Series race	10
Chase for the Cup	Win a championship in Season mode on the Car of Tomorrow Series Full Schedule	25
Earn Your Stripes	Earn your license for The Chase mode	25
Independent Contractor	Earn a contract in The Chase mode	25
Licensed to Drive	Complete all licenses in The Chase mode	25
Online Horsepower	Win an online race	25

Achievement	How to Earn It	Points
Toyota Reward	Complete all Toyota challenges	50
Craftsman Tools Reward	Save a Craftsman Tools Car setup for any track	50
Sprint Reward	Win a NEXTEL Cup in Season Mode on the NEXTEL Cup Series 2007 schedule	75
We Don't Need No Badges!	Earn all driver badges	100
Full Throttle	Complete a 100% Length Race in Race Now or Season Mode	100
Cross Country	Drive 5,000 miles	100
All or Nothing	Attain 100% Game progress	100
Chase Champion	Win a NEXTEL Cup in The Chase mode	100
Pay the Bills	Complete all Contracts in The Chase mode	100

NASCAR 09

XBOX 360

Make Your Car Exceed 200 MPH!

If you want to open the Kid Dyno-mite Xbox Gamerscore achievement, you must exceed 200 mph on a racetrack in any game mode. Most experienced racers will tell you to customize your car setup and choose a track

with a long straightaway like Pocono or Michigan Speedway, but here's a simpler solution:

✚ Turn off the Braking Assists feature at the Difficulty Settings menu.

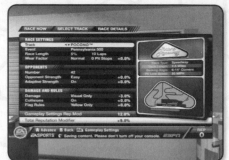

The Braking Assists feature is there to help you identify where to brake when you're going into a turn so you can avoid hitting a wall. However, you don't need to worry about walls if you're going for this achievement. Your goal is to reach 201 mph at any point on the track, and with Braking Assists on you'll rarely top 189 mph.

Tip: *Once you're familiar with the game and tracks, consider turning off the Braking Assists for other game achievements. You'll earn better lap times—you'll also find that disabling Braking Assists is the easiest way to beat Ryan Newman in the Sprint Driver Challenge mode!*

NASCAR 09 Xbox LIVE Gamerscore Achievements

Achievement	How to Earn It	Points
Keep On Truckin'	Win a race in the Craftsman Truck Series against at least 11 other racers	10
Nationwide Reward	Win a race in the Nationwide Series Championship against at least 11 other racers	10
Sprint Ahead	Win a race in the Sprint Cup Series against at least 11 other racers	10
Craftsman Champion	Win the Craftsman Truck Series Championship in Career mode	25
Top of the World	Own 100-rated Performance Point cars for all track types	25
Nationwide Champion	Win the Nationwide Championship in Career mode	25
Unfriendly	Take track ownership status from a friend	10
Chase for the Cup	Qualify for Chase for the Cup in Career mode	50
Chase Champion	Win the Sprint Cup Series Championship in Career mode	50
Are You Experienced?	Win a Sprint Driver Challenge event	10
Experience Wanted	Win 10 Sprint Driver Challenge events	25
The Ultimate Experience	Complete all Sprint Driver Challenge events	75
Mach 1	Earn a 761 point Rep Rating	25
Movin' On Up	Earn a 3,000 point Rep Rating	50
To the Top	Earn a 5,500 Rep Rating	100
Custom Car Creator	Complete a Custom Car for all racing series	10
Trade Your Setup	Upload a car setup to EA Locker	10

Achievement	How to Earn It	Points
We're Talkin' About Practice	Record a lap in Test and Tune mode	10
Kid Dyno-mite	Achieve a top speed of 200'mph	10
Worst to First	Win a race after starting in last place (you must have at least 11 opponents)	10
Online Horsepower	Win a Ranked Race on Xbox LIVE	50
Cross Country	Drive 5,000 total miles	75
Move Over Jeff	Win 82 races	25
Chase for the Cups	Win eight Sprint Cups in Career mode	100
King Me	Win 201 races total	200

NBA 2K6
XBOX 360

Earn 1,000 Points!
Because NBA 2K6 and College Hoops 2K6 are similar and offer nearly identical controller functions, you'll find that it's easy to transition from earning 1,000 Gamerscore Achievements in one 2K6 basketball game to the next.

+ To run up good numbers for multiple Gamerscore achievements, choose one of the perfect-rated (ranked at 100 points in defense and offense) teams like the Western Conference

All-Stars. Choose the Toronto Raptors as your opponent, because they have the lowest overall ratings and lowest defense rating.

+ Before you start a game, go to the Options menu and adjust the Game sliders so you always have three-point success, block success, and rip success. If you really want to make the game easy, you can reduce the sliders for the away team—but the game between the Western Conference

All-Stars and the Toronto Raptors is already a colossal mismatch, even if you choose the default game settings.

+ At the Options menu, you'll also find the Gameplay settings. Slide the difficulty sliders down to Rookie difficulty and turn off the Fatigue and Injuries options. Crank up the Quarter Length to a full 12 minutes, and you might be able to fulfill all of your Gamerscore achievements in a single game!

+ While you're at the Options menu, drop down to the NBA Rules menu and turn off the Charging, Blocking, Reaching, and Shooting fouls. Be sure to disable the Goaltending penalties, too. Now you're ready to add another 1,000 points to your Xbox Gamerscore!

Get a Triple-Double   250 points

What's a triple-double? That's when a player earns double-digit points in three of these five categories: points, steals, assists, rebounds, and blocked shots. If you set the Quarter Length in the game to 12 minutes, there's a good chance that you'll have several players with triple-doubles before the game is over. You improve your chances by making sure that your three-point shooter is also stealing for the entire team, especially if you max out your Rip Success, Pick Success, and Three-Point Success ratings at the Game Sliders menu. To seal the statistical deal before the end of the game, have the three-point shooter pass to the other players for at least ten assists.

Score 50 Points with Any Player
150 points

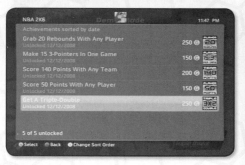

If you have a three-point shooter making 15 three-pointers in a game, that will get him to 45 points, so if you just complete two more three-pointers, you'll make this achievement with no problems. Remember to adjust your Three-Point Success ratings at the Game Sliders Menu and extend the Quarter Length in the game to 12 minutes. This way, you'll have no problem completing this achievement in the first quarter.

Score 140 Points with Any Team
200 points

With the Three-Point Success ratings maxed on the Game Sliders menu and the Quarter Length set to 12 minutes, you'll probably reach 140 points before the half.

Make 15 Three-pointers in One Game
150 points

If you set the sliders to the same settings outlined for getting the triple-double Gamerscore achievement, you'll have no problem earning this achievement before the end of the first quarter. Just remember to feed the ball to one player (someone like Kobe Bryant) and then let him take the shots. Once the Three-Point Success rating at the Game Sliders menu is maxed, you'll probably notice that you can make three-pointers from quite a distance behind the three-point line. Don't go too far back—most shots near mid-court will still miss the basket.

Grab 20 Rebounds with Any Player
250 points

Once you earn 140 points, pause the game and return to the Game Sliders menu. Now adjust the Three-Point Success slider all the way down to nothing. While it's unlikely that your players will hit from the three-point line, you can still steal the ball and earn offensive rebounds from your missed shots. Just be sure to attempt the three-pointers whenever you have players in or near the paint. If you set the Quarter Length in

the game to 12 minutes, several of your players will probably have at least 20 rebounds before the final buzzer sounds.

Tip: *Unlocking all of these accomplishments will also net you a ton of NBA 2K6 Crib Points that you can use to add new furnishings to your rooftop Crib. Check it out at the Features menu.*

NBA LIVE 09
XBOX 360, PLAYSTATION 3, PSP

Best Team Picks for Dynasty Mode

If you're going to win big (or if you want to simulate some games for an easy winning season), these powerhouse teams are the best choices for NBA LIVE 09's Dynasty Mode:

Dallas Mavericks	The Mavericks have the highest overall NBA rating in the game.
Phoenix Suns	Shaq is a year older, but still one of the best beneath the basket.
Houston Rockets	The combo of Yao Ming and Tracy McGrady make this team a contender.
Boston Celtics	Kevin Garnett, Paul Pierce, and Ray Allan are an exceptional power trio.
Utah Jazz	You can improve the Jazz by trading Ronnie Brewer for a stronger Shooting Guard.
Los Angeles Lakers	Kobe Bryant remains the highest rated player in NBA LIVE this season.

The Sprite Promotion Is Over! How Do I Get Super Dunks Mode?

Shortly after the release of NBA LIVE 09, you could find the code for Super Dunks Mode inside Sprite bottle caps. If you go to the Sprite vending machine at the NBA LIVE Academy gym, you can activate this mode by entering: **SPRITESLAM**

NBA LIVE 09 Xbox LIVE Gamerscore Achievements

Achievement	How to Earn It	Points
Ice Water	Win a solo game against the computer in overtime	30
Well-Rounded Player	Earn a triple double against the computer in Be a Pro mode	50
Super GM	Completely upgrade all of your team staff in Dynasty Mode	100
Perimeter Man	Complete all of the Guard Station challenges at NBA LIVE academy	50

LEBRON
JAMES
CAVALIERS
23 SMALL FORWARD

Achievement	How to Earn It	Points
BMOC	Complete all of the Big Man Station challenges at NBA LIVE academy	50
Team Player	Complete all of the Team-Play Station challenges at NBA LIVE academy	50
Created a monster	Use a created player and score over 60 points in a solo game against the computer	25
The Past is Present	Win a solo NBA LIVE Rewind game against the computer	25
Game of the Week	Plan and win the Game of the Week in matched online play	30
BAP MVP	Earn an 80 or higher against the computer in Be a Pro mode	30
David and Goliath	Using Superstar difficulty against the computer, defeat a team in Solo Match that is rated 10 points or higher than your team	50

Achievement	How to Earn It	Points
MVP	Have a player on your Dynasty Mode team win MVP for the regular season	30
NBA Finals MVP	Have a player from your Dynasty Mode team win the MVP award in the NBA Finals	30
All-Star	Have a player from your Dynasty Mode team earn a spot at the NBA All-Star Game	20

Achievement	How to Earn It	Points
All-NBA	Have a player from your Dynasty Mode team make the All-NBA team	20
Clutch	Make two free throws with less than two minutes to play against the computer at Superstar difficulty	20
G.O.A.T.	Win by at least 20 points against the computer at Superstar difficulty	60
The Comeback Kid	Go down 20 points in a solo mode game against the computer, then rally and win	40
Shock the World	Beat the computer and Team USA in a solo match at the FIBA World Championship tournament	30
The Grinder	Participate in 20 online ranked games	100
Club Victory	Play and win in Team Play Club mode	50
Cool Off	Using at least 10-minute quarters against the computer, shut down a player with a Shot Streak and keep his point total under 10 points	50
Old School	Win a solo game without using a dunk or a three-point shot against the computer	60

OPEN SEASON

XBOX 360

Unlock the Mini Games!

You can access the Open Season Mini Games by completing specific levels in Open Season:

NEW MINI-GAME!

You've unlocked a new mini-game!

ALL RIGHT!

To Open Mini Game	Complete This Level
Duck Chorus	Crazy Quackers
Flowers for my Deer	Meet the Skunks
Rise, Rise to the Top	Beaver Damage
Shake that Butt!	Hunted level
Wild Memory	Shaw's Shack

Open Season Gamerscore Achievements

Achievement	How to Earn It	Points
Acorns Badges!	Collect all 10 Acorn Badges	15
Adventure Completed!	Complete the adventure	50
Beetle Badges!	Collect all 10 Beetle Badges	15
Buddy with all animals!	Become a buddy with all animals	15
Buddy with Beavers!	Become a buddy with the beavers	5
Buddy with Deer!	Become a buddy with the deer	5
Buddy with Ducks!	Become a buddy with the ducks	5

A B C D E F G H I J K L M N O P Q R S T U V W X Y Z

Achievement	How to Earn It	Points
Buddy with Porcupines!	Become a buddy with the porcupines	5
Buddy with Rabbits!	Become a buddy with the rabbits	5
Buddy with Skunks!	Become a buddy with the skunks	5
Buddy with Squirrels!	Become a buddy with the squirrels	5
Butterfly Badges!	Collect all 10 Butterfly Badges	15
Collection Rewards!	Unlock all 10 collection rewards	100
Feather Badges!	Collect all 10 Feather Badges	15
Leaf Badges!	Collect all 10 Leaf Badges	15
Maximum Wild Obtained!	Complete the game with maximum Wild Points	100
Mushrooms Badges!	Collect all 10 Mushroom Badges	15
Perfect Beaver Damage!	Complete Beaver Damage with maximum Wild Points	20
Perfect Chainsaw Cha Cha!	Complete Chainsaw Cha Cha with maximum Wild Points	20

Achievement	How to Earn It	Points
Perfect Clear the Ducks!	Complete Clear the Ducks with maximum Wild Points	20
Perfect Crazy Quackers!	Complete Crazy Quackers with maximum Wild Points	20
Perfect Dinkelman Dreams!	Complete Dinkelman Dreams with maximum Wild Points	20
Perfect Duck and Cover!	Complete Duck and Cover with maximum Wild Points	20
Perfect for Hoof It!	Complete Hoof It with maximum Wild Points	20
Perfect Fowl Duty!	Complete Fowl Duty with maximum Wild Points	20
Perfect Meet the Skunks!	Complete Meet the Skunks with maximum Wild Points	20
Perfect Mine Shafted!	Complete Mine Shafted with maximum Wild Points	20

Achievement	How to Earn It	Points
Perfect Protect the Clan's Tree!	Complete Protect the Clan's Tree with maximum Wild Points	20
Perfect Puni Mart Picnic!	Complete Puni Mart Picnic with maximum Wild Points	20
Perfect Reilly's Rampage!	Complete Reilly's Rampage with maximum Wild Points	20
Perfect Rocky River!	Complete Rocky River with maximum Wild Points	20
Perfect Scare Bear!	Complete Scare Bear with maximum Wild Points	20
Perfect Shaw Showdown!	Complete Shaw Showdown with maximum Wild Points	20
Perfect Shaw's Shack!	Complete Shaw's Shack with maximum Wild Points	20
Perfect Snow Blitz!	Complete Snow Blitz with maximum Wild Points	20
Perfect Start the Battle!	Complete Start the Battle with maximum Wild Points	20
Perfect Tanks a Lot!	Complete Tanks a Lot with maximum Wild Points	20
Perfect Timberline!	Complete Timberline with maximum Wild Points	20
Perfect Toothy Torpedoes!	Complete Toothy Torpedoes with maximum Wild Points	20
Perfect Trouble with Trappers!	Complete Trouble with Trappers with maximum Wild Points	20
Perfect Wake in the Wild!	Complete Wake in the Wild with maximum Wild Points	20
Track Badges!	Collect all 10 Track Badges	15
Trash Badges!	Collect all 10 Trash Badges	15
Wild Skills!	Master all 15 Wild Skills.	65

Garage Games

Look inside the garage where you choose your ride. Scroll down past "More…" at the bottom of the menu. Choose it and then select "Walk around this garage." Inside the garage you can play demos of Geometry Wars and Geometry Wars Retro. If you play both of these games, you'll unlock the Arcade Player Gamerscore Achievement!

Kudos for Concept Cars

Before you can buy a concept car, you must earn Kudos to unlock it. Kudos are points that you earn by pulling off a move during a race. Kudo-earning moves include jumps, spins, passes, drifts, and driving a clean section on a race course. You can add Combo Bonuses to your Kudo Stash by quickly executing several Kudo moves in a single race—as long as you don't hit obstacles or other racers. When you earn enough Kudos, you'll unlock a concept car. Use

your racing credits to buy these concept cars. Here's the list of concept cars and the number of Kudos required to unlock each one:

Concept Car	Kudos
Ford Mustang GTR	10,000
Nissan GTR	50,000
Cadillac 16	90,000
Ford Supercar Concept	120,000
Shelby Cobra	160,000
Toyota GT-One	230,000
Ford GT90	300,000
Shelby GR-1	390,000
RUF Supercar Concept	475,000

Project Gotham Racing 3 Xbox 360 Gamerscore Achievements

Achievement	How to Earn It	Points
Arcade Player	Play both arcade games inside the garage	15
Track Builder	Design and save ten custom routes	10
Photographer	Take a picture in each city and save your shot	10
Gotham TV Sports Fan	Save a Gotham TV replay and watch it 10 times	15
Gotham Hero	Be the feature on Gotham TV	30
Race Against the Clock	Set a lap time in Race Against the Clock mode for every course	50
Ferrari Owners Club	Buy all Ferrari models in the game	45
Lamborghini Owners Club	Buy all Lamborghini models in the game	45
Exotic Car Club	Collect all the exotic models in the game	45
Steel Champion	Complete all Steel level championships	30
Bronze Champion	Complete all Bronze level championships	50
Silver Champion	Complete all Silver level championships	60
Gold Champion	Complete all Gold level championships	75
Platinum Champion	Complete all Platinum level championships	100
Style Racer Badge	Earn kudos for every move, plus a 10x Combo, 25,000 Kudo points, 1,000 Kudos in a single race and execute a powerslide for at least 25 meters	50

Achievement	How to Earn It	Points
Pro Racer Badge	Win a Platinum medal while using the manual transmission option	60
Online Professional	Run a clean online race, qualify last and finish first, maintain a three-race winning streak, earn a clean race, and participate in at least 50 online races	60
Tournament Qualifier	Make it to the first elimination round in a tournament	50
Rank 10	Attain Rank 10	20
Rank 5	Attain Rank 5	50
Rank 1	Attain Rank 1	80
Mouse Master	Use an E-Class car to win a Cat & Mouse event	15
Cat Champion	Use a car that isn't an E-Class to win a Cat & Mouse event	10
Cone Capture Champion	Win a Cone Capture contest	15
Team Cone Capture Champion	Be on a team that wins a Team Cone Capture contest	10

PROJECT GOTHAM RACING 4
XBOX 360

Sometimes the Target Finishing Position Isn't the Target

Depending on the difficulty level you choose, some of the early races in Gotham Career mode can be tough until you get a better car. In situations where the target finishing position is third, lock in your finishing position by knocking one

of your opponents into the railings—but don't hit anything in the middle of tricks or you'll lose Kudos! The easiest way is bump a motorcycle racer so he has to jump on his bike again, but you can also do it to other motorists by pushing them into railings. If you do this on the last lap of the race, your opponent will have a tough time catching you before the finish line.

Project Gotham Racing 4 Xbox LIVE Gamerscore Achievements

Achievement	How to Earn It	Points
Winning Streak	Win three back-to-back races in Arcade or Single-player mode	30
1-2 Finish	Win the top two finishing positions in a Racked Match Team Championship	10
Team Domination	Finish a Ranked Match Team Championship with team members in the top four finishing spots	20
Team Leader	Earn the most points on your team in a Ranked Match Team Championship	10
Showboater	Earn 9,000 Kudos in a race	20
5-Star Racer	Earn 5 Kudo stars	20
Superstar	Earn 5 Kudo stars three times in a single race event	40
Mind Your Manners	Win a race in Gotham Career or Arcade Mode without touching a wall or barrier	25

Achievement	How to Earn It	Points
The Unicyclist	Execute a long wheelie with a motorbike	20
Bibendum	Play all three Test Tracks and set a score on each one	10
Weather Master	Win a race in fog, snow, or rain in Career or Arcade modes	25
Winner	Win an event in Career or Arcade mode	5

Achievement	How to Earn It	Points
Silver Gotham Arcader	Earn Silver Medals in all Arcade mode events	10
Gold Gotham Arcader	Earn Gold Medals in all Arcade mode events	10
Platinum Gotham Arcader	Earn Platinum Medals in all Arcade mode events	10
Silver Double	Earn a Silver medal or more with a bike and a car in Arcade mode	30
Gold Double	Earn a Gold medal or more with a bike and a car in Arcade mode	5
Platinum Double	Earn a Platinum medal with a bike and a car in Arcade mode	5
Arcade Chapter Complete	Complete any Arcade mode chapter	30
Professional	Attain professional rank in Career mode	70
Hotshot	Attain Hotshot rank in Career mode	70
Master	Attain Master rank in Career mode	40
Hero	Attain National Champion rank in Career mode	20
Champion	Win your first championship in Career mode or Ranked match play	10
Motorcycle Ace	Win a championship in Career mode on a motorbike	25
Major Winner	Win a Major in Career mode	40
Dominator	Win all three Single-Player Career Majors	40
Stuntman	Perform a stunt on a motorbike	5
Buy an Achievement	Buy the million-Kudo Gamer picture	20

Achievement	How to Earn It	Points
Back it Up!	Finish 1st and 2nd in reverse gear against an AI opponent in a split-screen Street Race	10
Strike a Pose	Face two bikes at least 15 meters apart and do Endo moves	10
First Timer	Complete your first Ranked Match Championship	10
8th Wonder of the World	Complete a lap while sliding on the Michelin Figure-8 test track	20
Catch 'Em All	Trade paint by hitting every opponent in an eight-vehicle race	5
Endo King	Earn 100 Kudos doing an Endo move on a motorbike	20
Seat of Your Pants	Finish a Hot Lap in Arcade mode without ever braking	25

Achievement	How to Earn It	Points
Rubbin' is Racin'	Knock the wing mirrors off every rival car in single-player Street Race	20
Show Jump	Race in an event where eight vehicles are airborne simultaneously	10
I Love PGR	Buy everything in the PGR Shop or finish PGR3 ranked #1	5
Whitewash	Win all events in a Single-player or Ranked Match Championship	50
You Won't Believe Your Eyes!	Create a 3-D image in Photo Mode	5
Secret Agent	Complete Puzzle #2	5
3CZV657	Complete Puzzle #1	5
Tonight Make Me Unstoppable	Complete Puzzle #3	5
Play It Again, Sam	Improve any medal already earned in Arcade mode	20
PGR on Demand - Photo	Upload a photo and vote for photos at PGR On Demand	5
PGR on Demand - Video	Upload a replay and vote for replays at PGR On Demand	5
Giant Killer	Win against another player with Rank 1 status on Xbox LIVE	20
Numero Uno	Reach Rank 1 on the Career Driver's Leaderboard	50
Beat Bizarre	Beat a PGR4 development team member on Xbox Live or beat any other player who defeated a PGR4 development team member	10

Xbox LIVE Premium Downloadable Accomplishments:

Achievement	How to Earn It	Points
Tourist Kudos King	Earn the most Kudos in a Tourist event	15
Open Cat Champion	Be a cat and win a Cat and Mouse Open event	15
Open Mouse Master	Be a mouse and win a Cat and Mouse Open event	15
Platinum Plus	Earn all the Platinum medals in the Platinum Plus Challenge event	60
Download King	Finish the DLC Challenge at all difficulties	60
Arcade Challenge	Finish the Arcade Challenge at all difficulties	50
Cheater	Activate a cheat in the Cheat Menu	5
Make the Grade	Try to qualify for a Tournament	10
01 Yee Haw	Solve Puzzle #4	10
Are You the One?	Solve Puzzle #5	10

While most Xbox 360 games feature 1000 Gamerscore Achievement points, the list for Project Gotham Racing 4 adds up to 1,250 points because it includes downloadable content! You must buy and download the PGR4 Premium Challenge Pack on Xbox Live. You can check for downloadable content by choosing Xbox Live Marketplace at the Project Gotham Racing 4 main menu.

PURE

XBOX 360, PLAYSTATION 3

Three Important Ways to Win World Tour Mode

Adding ATV upgrades is important for winning in World Tour mode, but most players find themselves falling behind if they try to create one do-it-all ATV for winning every event. The most popular strategy among experienced racers is to unlock and build three distinct ATVs:

+ A Freestyle ATV equipped with parts for high stats in Tricks and Handling
+ A Race ATV equipped with parts for high stats in Max Speed and Handling
+ A Sprint ATV equipped with parts for high stats in Acceleration and Handling

As you win races and unlock more parts, fit the parts that improve your specific performance in your specialized ATVs. The extra time you spend modifying your ATVs will save you hours of frustration on the trickier courses—and that's more time you can spend winning or looking for hidden shortcuts!

PURE Xbox LIVE Gamerscore Achievements

Achievement	How to Earn It	Points
Finished an Event	Complete an event in the game at any difficulty	5
Unlocked Stage 2	Unlock Stage 2	5
Unlocked Stage 3	Unlock Stage 3	5

Achievement	How to Earn It	Points
Unlocked Stage 4	Unlock Stage 4	5
Unlocked Stage 5	Unlock Stage 5	10
Unlocked Stage 6	Unlock Stage 6	10
Unlocked Stage 7	Unlock Stage 7	10
Unlocked Stage 8	Unlock Stage 8	10
Unlocked Stage 9	Unlock Stage 9	10
Unlocked Stage 10	Unlock Stage 10	10
Completed Stage 1	Finish first in all four Stage 1 events	10
Completed Stage 2	Finish first in all four Stage 2 events	20
Completed Stage 3	Finish first in all four Stage 3 events	20
Completed Stage 4	Finish first in all four Stage 4 events	20
Completed Stage 5	Finish first in all five Stage 5 events	20
Completed Stage 6	Finish first in all five Stage 6 events	20
Completed Stage 7	Finish first in all five Stage 7 events	20

Achievement	How to Earn It	Points
Completed Stage 8	Finish first in all six Stage 8 events	30
Completed Stage 9	Finish first in all six Stage 9 events	30
Completed Stage 10	Finish first in all seven Stage 10 events	50
1 of a Kind	Build an ATV from scratch at the garage	5
Fully Loaded	Unlock and fill the ATV slots in the garage	10
Mechanic	Build five ATVs and make sure all have different engines	10
Flawless Lap	Finish a lap in any World Tour mode race without falling off your ride	5
Flawless Event	Finish a World Tour mode event without falling off your ride	10

Achievement	How to Earn It	Points
Tricked Out	Perform all of the normal tricks in the game during a single World Tour mode event	20
Specialized	Perform eight different special tricks during a single World Tour mode event	25
Freestyler	Extend a Freestyle event past the third lap	30
Triple Flip	Perform a 1080-degree rotation (forward or backwards) during a jump	20
Nice Combo!	Perform a combo worth 50,000 points during an event	10
Sick Combo!	Perform a combo worth 125,000 points during an event	20
Killer Combo!	Perform a combo worth 250,000 points during an event	30
You're Special!	Perform every trick in the game during an event	20
Pure Perfection	Finish first in every event in Pure World Tour mode	100
Grease Monkey	Finish first in World Tour mode while using every engine type once	25
Comeback Kid	Start or advance from last place and win a World Tour mode race	10
Fresh Air	Win a Freestyle event using only Fresh tricks	20
No Messing	Participate in 42 events and complete World Tour mode	25

Achievement	How to Earn It	Points
Zero to Hero	Earn a special trick within 30 seconds after a race start	20
You Reckon?	Perform a special trick during a single-player Sprint event	20
Two Time!	Perform two special tricks during one jump	25
Hang Time!	During a race, spend an accumulated 150 seconds airborne and still win the race	25
Learner Driver	Lap a rival in a single-player Sprint event	25
No Pain, No Gain	Crash at least 11 times and still win an online Race or Sprint event	25
Full Speed Ahead	Keep the accelerator down throughout an entire online Race or Sprint event	25
Show Off	Do a wheelie as you cross the finish line on every lap before you win an online Race or Sprint event	20
Win Online	Finish first in an online event	10
5 in a Row	Finish first in five online events in a row	30
Underdog	Use an ATV with a Class D engine to beat a rival with a Class A engine in a ranked online match	30
Online Champ	Finish first in an online championship event	30

Brake Before the Turns, but Don't Sweat Most Gravel Detours

Like Grid, Gran Turismo Prelude, and Forza Motosports 2, Race Pro emphasizes straight-line braking before sharp turns, so it's important to slow down before going into the turns. Otherwise, you'll end up skidding and possibly taking a trip off track.

The big difference between Race Pro and other racing games is that you won't slow down much when you drive off the track and into the gravel—at least in Career Mode's Novice and Semi-Pro difficulty levels. If you skid off-road on courses like Curitiba or Anderstorp, keep your foot on the gas and steer your way back onto the course before other cars can catch up. In some cases, a quick excursion through a gravel trap might give you three extra seconds over your competition, but if you take a large off-road detour, you'll be penalized for cutting the track! At the Professional level, you'll find that your racing rivals quickly catch up whenever you drive off the course.

What Do the Numbers above Each Turn Mean?

Whenever you approach a turn on any racecourse, you'll see

an arrow appear with a number next to it. These arrows and numbers show you the direction of the turn and the gear you should be in to navigate the corner. If you're not sure which gear you're in, it's the large number in the middle of the tachometer dial in the lower right corner—the one just above your speed display.

If you want to win on the Professional difficulty setting, consider these gear/corner numbers as guidelines, not rules, especially when you move into the more advanced cars like the Formula BMW open-wheel cars. At the Professional level, your opponents are extremely fast, so push your luck and skill by taking these tricky turns in higher gears, but you'll wear down your tires faster in long races than you would during short sprints.

Patience Is the Winning Strategy

At all difficulty levels in Race Pro, you'll race against aggressive computer-controlled rival drivers. Your chances of a wreck are much higher on courses with a tight or close first turn near the starting line. Examples of these courses in the early levels include Brands Hatch, Anderstorp, Zandervoort, Oschersleben, and Laguna Seca. Keep these dangerous early turns in mind when you're racing. If you're not in pole position and you can't get away cleanly, don't try threading the needle by weaving through traffic—your rivals will cut you off, intentionally spin you, or possibly damage your car. Instead, keep

your place in the pack through the first early turn and let the other drivers sort things out. Then, push hard to pass everyone on the first or second long straightaway. This patient strategy gives you the edge in the races—and the game!

Race Pro Xbox LIVE Gamerscore Achievements

Achievement	How to Earn It	Points
On Call	Complete a stand-in race	10
All or Nothing	Complete a tryout	10
Trophy Owner	Complete a contract with full points	20
Contracted	Complete a contract	10
Time Chaser	Complete a full lap in Time Attack mode	10
Fast Learner	Beat the ghost car in Time Attack mode	10
Qualifier	Complete a qualifying session	10
Front Man	Get pole position with Novice difficulty	5
Pace Setter	Get pole position in Semi-pro difficulty	10
Pole Sitter	Get pole position in Professional difficulty	15
Novice Winner	Win a race in Novice difficulty	10
Front Runner	Win a race in Semi-pro difficulty	15
Like a Pro	Win a race in Professional difficulty	20
Clean Conscience	Win a race in Professional difficulty without damaging your car	25
Championship Contender	Complete a full championship	20
The Champ	Finish 1st in a championship	30
Champ for Life	Finish 1st in a championship in Profession difficulty	40
Racing Icon	Finish all championships	50

Achievement	How to Earn It	Points
Trophy Collector	Complete all contracts with full points	50
Clean Sweep	Complete all contracts in Career mode	30
Race Initiator	Host a multiplayer race on Xbox LIVE	10
Race Generator	Host 50 multiplayer races on Xbox LIVE	30
Event Creator	Host a ranked multiplayer match on Xbox LIVE	10
Race Promoter	Host 50 ranked multiplayer matches on Xbox LIVE	30
Club Racer	Finish a multiplayer match on Xbox LIVE	10
Veteran Club Racer	Finish 50 multiplayer matches on Xbox LIVE	25
Xbox LIVE Race Driver	Complete an Xbox LIVE ranked match	10
Xbox LIVE veteran	Complete 50 Xbox LIVE ranked matches	25
Proven Winner	Finish 1st in an Xbox LIVE ranked match	20
Player Match Winner	Finish 1st in an Xbox LIVE player match	20
Club Icon	Finish 1st 50 times in an Xbox LIVE player match	50
Legendary	Finish 1st 50 times in an Xbox LIVE ranked match	50
Team Racer	Complete a cooperative HotSeat game	10
Social Racer	Complete a competitive HotSeat game	10
Team Win	Win a cooperative HotSeat game	10

Achievement	How to Earn It	Points
Ownage	Win a competitive HotSeat game	10
Monza Win	Finish 1st on Monza at Professional difficulty	20
Brno Win	Finish 1st on Brno at Professional difficulty	20
Oschersleben Win	Finish 1st on Oschersleben at Professional difficulty	20
Macau Win	Finish 1st on Macau at Professional difficulty	20
Pau Win	Finish 1st on Pau at Professional difficulty	20
Porto Win	Finish 1st on Porto at Professional difficulty	20
Zandvoort Win	Finish 1st on Zandvoort at Professional difficulty	20
Brands Hatch Win	Finish 1st on Brands Hatch at Professional difficulty	20
Curitiba Win	Finish 1st on Curitiba at Professional difficulty	20
Valencia Win	Finish 1st on Valencia at Professional difficulty	20
Anderstorp Win	Finish 1st on Anderstorp at Professional difficulty	20
Laguna Seca Win	Finish 1st on Laguna Seca at Professional difficulty	20
Road America Win	Finish 1st on Road America at Professional difficulty	20
Apex Hunter	Finish 1st in any race with a custom car setup	10

REEL FISHING: ANGLER'S DREAM

NINTENDO WII

Know What You Need to Catch to Reach the Next Stage

If you know what you're trying to catch in Reel Fishing, Angler's Dream, you'll quickly move through the stages in the game. Outlined below are the target goals for all of the fishing locations.

Stage	Target Fish
Lake	Catch three fish.
Midstream	Catch four Pale Chubs.
Rocky Coast	Catch a Parrotfish and a Black Porgy.
Mountain Stream	Catch a Yamame Trout and a River Mackerel
Back to the Lake	Catch the Golden Black Bass!
Open Sea	Catch a Yellowtail Tuna larger than 71 inches.
Upstream	Catch a Rainbow Trout and a Sakura Trout.
Pond	Catch a Deepbodied Crucian Carp larger than 14 inches.
Beach	Catch at least five Bonefish.
Back Upstream	Catch the Brilliant Rainbow Trout
Headwaters	Catch at least two Char that are larger than 18 inches.
Downstream	Catch at least six Pink Salmon.
South Seas	Catch three Giant Trevally and three Dorado.

Note: *You don't have to catch all of your target fish for a stage in a single day. You can always return to your fishing spot and try again the next morning.*

How and Where to Find the Legendary Fish

Fish:	Location:	To Encounter:	To Land:
Legendary Catfish	Lake	Catch ten fish with the Bass Rod	Play for at least one hour
Legendary Brook Trout	Midstream	Catch ten fish with the Fly Rod	Catch at least 30 fish
Legendary Parrotfish	Coast	Catch ten fish with the Coast Rod	Own at least 41 lures
Legendary Yamame Trout	Mountain Stream	Catch ten fish with the Mountain Stream Rod	Release at least 20 fish
Legendary Bluefin Tuna	Open Sea	Catch ten fish with the Boat Rod	Catch at least 51 fish in the game
Legendary Brown Trout	Upstream	Catch ten fish with the Trout Rod	Play at least four hours
Legendary Crucian Carp	Pond	Catch ten fish with the Carp Rod	Catch at least 31 different types of fish

This is my secret fishing spot, the Mountain Lake.
I'll let you to find out what fish live here on
your own!

The fish got away.
What was that giant fish...?

Fish:	Location:	To Encounter:	To Land:
Legendary Tarpon	Beach	Catch ten fish with the Shore Rod	Own 81 lures
Legendary Char	Headwaters	Catch ten fish with the Mountain Stream Rod	Play through a year in the game.
Legendary King Salmon	Downstream	Catch ten fish with the Fly Rod	Play at least eight hours of game time
Legendary Blue Marlin	South Seas	Catch ten fish with the Off-Shore Rod	Catch at least 100 fish in the game
Great King Huchen	Hidden Fishing Spot	Catch ten fish with the Trout Rod	Catch the 11 legendary fish

After you encounter a legendary fish for the first time, you must return to the Aqua Lodge and learn more about the fish from the white-haired guide. After the guide tells you about the fish, you can return to the fishing location and try your luck!

SEGA RALLY REVO
XBOX 360

Unlock the Secret No-Collision Achievement!

Some video game racers consider SEGA Rally Revo to be one of the toughest racing games released on the Xbox 360, but

this arcade racing title rewards smart players who use strategy to win and unlock achievements! The secret no-collision achievement is worth a whopping 80 points, so it's worth the extra effort: Practice driving (and winning!) Safari 1 in the AZA Challenge stage. This

is the first course you'll encounter in the game and one of the widest (even at the single hairpin turn), so most drivers find that it's the easiest to win.

Note: *You could also drive the hairpin-free Canyon 1 if you prefer that course instead, but the Alpine 1 course features three narrow hairpin turns that almost guarantee a collision with nearby rival drivers.*

You're trying to avoid hitting other drivers to win this achievement, so don't crowd the other racers at the start. Your goal is to pass each racer carefully one at a time, so avoid the jostling right after the start line—but don't allow your rivals to drive away with a huge lead.

Tip: *As you work your way through the pack, avoid the driving line (the skid marks where other drivers were driving) and you'll find it easier to stay away from the other cars. Avoiding the driver's line will also take you around some of the big water obstacles that slow down other cars, and help you avoid the slick sections where other vehicles ripped up the mud on previous laps.*

If you time your moves right, you should be leading everyone— without a single dent to your car—on the final lap!

SEGA Rally Revo Xbox LIVE Gamerscore Achievements

Achievement	How to Earn It	Points
Premier Professional	Unlock Premier Professional League	5
Premier Expert	Unlock Premier Expert League	10
Premier Champion	Finish first in the Premier Final in Championship mode	20
Modified Amateur	Earn enough points in Championship mode to unlock Modified Amateur League	5
Modified Professional	Earn enough points in Championship mode to unlock Modified Professional League	10
Modified Expert	Earn enough points in Championship mode to unlock Modified Expert League	20
Modified Champion	Finish first in the Modified Final in Championship mode	30
Masters Amateur	Earn enough points in Championship mode to unlock the Masters Amateur League	10
Masters Professional	Earn enough points in Championship mode to unlock the Masters Professional League	20
Masters Expert	Earn enough points in Championship mode to unlock the Masters Expert League	30
Masters Champion	Finish first in the Master Final in Championship mode	40
Grand Slam	Finish first in every rally in Championship mode	50
Perfect Score	Finish first in every rally race in Championship mode	100

Achievement	How to Earn It	Points
Car Collector	Unlock all the cars in Championship mode	20
Livery Collector	Drive at least 50 miles in the first six unlocked cars in single-player Championship mode	20
Safari Expert	Finish first on all Safari tracks in any single-player mode	10
Lakeside Expert	Finish first on the Lakeside track in any single-player mode	10
Arctic Expert	Finish first on all Arctic tracks in any single-player mode	10
Alpine Expert	Finish first on all Alpine tracks in any single-player mode	10
Canyon Expert	Finish first on all Canyon tracks in any single-player mode	10
Tropical Expert	Finish first on all Tropical tracks in any single-player mode	10

Achievement	How to Earn It	Points
Tourist	Drive Drive at least 300 miles (480 kilometers) in single-player mode events	10
Trekker	Drive at least 500 miles (800 kilometers) in single-player mode events	20
Explorer	Drive at least 1,000 miles (1,600 kilometers) in single-player mode events	30
Off-Road Expert	Use the Off-Road setup option and win a Championship rally	10
Road Expert	Use the Road setup option and win a Championships rally	10
Manual Expert	Use the manual transmission and win a Championship rally	10
Safari Time Attack	Beat the target times for all car classes in every Safari track in Time Attack mode	20
Lakeside Time Attack	Beat the target times for all car classes in the Lakeside track in Time Attack mode	20
Arctic Time Attack	Beat the target times for all car classes in every Arctic track in Time Attack mode	20
Alpine Time Attack	Beat the target times for all car classes in every Alpine track in Time Attack mode	20
Canyon Time Attack	Beat the target times for all car classes in every Canyon track in Time Attack mode	20
Tropical Time Attack	Beat the target times for all car classes in every Tropical track in Time Attack mode	20
Head to Head	Race on all tracks in Head-to-Head mode	20

Achievement	How to Earn It	Points
Live Novice	Complete 10 races on Xbox LIVE	10
Live veteran	Complete 100 races on Xbox LIVE	30
5 ranked	Win five ranked races on Xbox LIVE	30
10 ranked	Win ten ranked races on Xbox LIVE	50
Social hoster	Host and finish at least 100 races on Xbox LIVE	30
Secret 1	Win a race without a collision with another car	80
Secret 2	Win a race while going backwards across the finish line	20
Secret 3	Exceed 160 mph (260 kpm)	20
Secret 4	Remain airborne for at least two seconds	30
Secret 5	Remain in first place at the end of the first lap	20

SETTLERS OF CATAN
XBOX 360

Favorite Winning Strategies Against Computer Players

Several key strategies for playing Settlers of Catan apply to both the Xbox 360 game and the real board game. In the Xbox version, it's important to remember that computer players will stop trading with you once you have a substantial lead. The trick is to keep the game close until you're in a position to build and earn victory points without relying on other players in the game!

Brick and Wood Strategy

Brick and ore are two rare commodities on the board, so place a settlement on a brick spot early and then grab a wood. Your strategy is to build roads and establish new settlements faster than your opponents—and the players who hold brick and wood on good numbers always expand quickest in the beginning of a game. Focus first on wood and brick hexes with the numbers 5, 6, 8, and 9. If you isolate one or more of your opponents, you can cut off their expansion and slow their progress. The brick and wood strategy is one of the most popular strategies used by new players, although it only works when your numbers are rolled more than other player's!

The City Strategy

You can build cities faster than other players if you place your starting settlements around

ore and grain hexes; however, you must rely on trading to acquire important commodities to build roads and additional settlements. If you're going to use this city-building strategy, it's a good idea to expand your road and settlement network before you build cities. This makes the beginning of the game a little tough. Computer players will be reluctant to trade with you once you're a couple of cities ahead of them. As you build roads, try putting a settlement on a sheep hex so you can add more development cards to your holdings.

The Development Card Strategy

Starting out with a large number of ore, grain, and sheep options allows you the freedom to buy development cards. It might also allow you to keep your total victory points hidden from the computer players. You can also use your ore and grain cards to build cities. But remember that your computer opponents can see these cities, and they'll stop trading with you if you gain a large lead. The Development Card strategy is a favorite among experienced players who know how to use all the cards in the deck. The soldier cards offer a great defense against the computer characters because they often slow you down by leaving the robber next to your most productive settlements and cities.

The Balanced Commodity Strategy

The balanced commodity strategy works only if the game rolls your numbers often. If you place your starting settlements next to brick, wood, grain, and sheep (or three of those commodities and a 3:1 port), you have a balance of materials for building roads and settlements. Some players push this advantage further by adding ore to their starting group, but it's difficult to start with all of these commodities on the first turn.

There's a danger of being isolated by players who build roads around you, cutting off your expansion options. If your numbers don't come up, you must trade with your computer opponents—but they won't be willing to make deals near the end of the game, so your strategy comes down to luck on the die rolls.

While there are other trading that strategies involving trading that players use in the board game, remember that your computer opponents won't be forced into unfavorable trades. If your strategy for

winning depends on trades late in the game, the only way the computer has a chance to win is by rejecting your trades and gambling on better numbers rolling on the next turn.

Settlers of Catan Xbox LIVE Gamerscore Achievements

Because Settlers of Catan is a download game, it offers only 200 Gamerscore achievement points instead of the 1,000 points found in most store titles.

Achievement	How to Earn It	Points
Settler of Catan	Build a settlement (aside from the two you start with) in any Catan game mode	10
Scholar of Catan	Win a single-player game on Moderate difficulty against three computer players	10
Villager of Catan	Earn 25 Victory Points in multiple single-player games	10
Ambassador of Catan	Invite another player to play Catan online	10
Builder of Catan	End (win or lose) ten games while possessing the Longest Road card	20
Knight of Catan	End (win or lose) ten games while possessing the Largest Army card	20

Achievement	How to Earn It	Points
Merchant of Catan	Draw 100 resource cards in any Catan game mode	20
Professor of Catan	Win a single-player game on Hard difficulty against three computer players	20
Citizen of Catan	Earn 100 Victory Points in multiple single-player games	20
Elder of Catan	Earn 250 Victory Points in multiple single-player games	20
Statesman of Catan	Earn 500 Victory Points in ranked match play	20
Chancellor of Catan	Earn 1,000 Victory Points in ranked match play	20

SIMCITY CREATOR

NINTENDO WII

Urban Unlocks

The following items unlock when you reach certain conditions in the game. Be patient! Sometimes it takes a few moments before the game recognizes and rewards you with a new achievement:

Feature	Condition
Art Museum	Education level at 90
Basketball Court	Build a pair of tennis courts, baseball fields, and playgrounds
Bus Stop	Reach the year 1920
Fusion Power Plant	Reach the year 2030
High School	Education level at 75
House of Worship	Population around 4,000
Large Garden	Population around 50,000 with four small gardens
Large Park	Population around 50,000 with four small parks
Mayor's House	Population around 22,000
Mayor's Statue	Population around 5,000
Museum	Education level at 100
Nuclear Power Plant	Education level at 115

Feature	Condition
Opera House	Construct a trio of museums and art museums
Recycling Plant	Designate a landfill zone
Soccer Field	Population around 70,000 with two tennis courts, two basketball courts and two playgrounds
Solar Power Plant	Reach the year 2000
Space Port	Reach the year 2050
Stadium	Population around 350,000
TV Station	Population around 350,000
University	Education level 90
Wind Power Plant	Reach the year 1985

SKATE IT

NINTENDO WII

Unlock the Pros in Career Mode!

Compete the following sponsorship challenges in Career mode and you'll unlock these pros:

Sponsorship Challenge	Character
Cliché	Lucas Puig
Plan B	Danny Way
Alien Workshop	Rob Dyrdek
Girl	Mike Carroll
Baker	Terry Kennedy
Almost	Chris Haslam
Blind	Jake Brown
Lakai	Eric Koston

SONIC UNLEASHED

WII, XBOX 360, PLAYSTATION 2, PLAYSTATION 3

The Best Times for S Ranks under the Sun!

The following Stage Clear times will earn you S-Rankings in the daylight stages of Sonic Unleashed:

Apotos Windmill Isle Act 1	1:10
Apotos Windmill Isle Act 2	3:30
Egg Beetle in Mazuri	2:20
Holoska Cool Edge	3:20
Spagonia Rooftop Run	2:50
Spagonia Dragon Road	3:10
Egg Devil Ray in Spagonia	3:40
Shamar Arid Sands	2:40
Adabat Jungle Joyride	2:15
Egg Lancer in Adabat	3:30
Eggmanland	4:30
Dark Gaia in Eggmanland	7:30

Sonic Unleashed Xbox LIVE Gamerscore Achievements

Achievement	How to Earn It	Points
Still Broken	Restore the first continent	25
Looking Better	Restore the second continent	25
Still a Jigsaw Puzzle	Restore the third continent	25
Picking Up the Pieces	Restore the fourth continent	25
Almost There	Restore the fifth continent	25
One More to Go	Restore the sixth continent	25
World Savior	Complete the Game	100
Partly Cloudy	Collect half of the Sun Medals in the game	30
Sunny	Collect all Sun Medals	50
Half Moon	Collect half of the Moon Medals in the game	30
Full Moon	Collect all Moon Medals	50
Blue Streak	Max out all Sonic the Hedgehog stats	30
Power Overwhelming	Max out all Sonic the Werehog stats	30
Getting the Hang of Things	Achieve an S Rank in a Sonic the Hedgehog stage	15
Creature of the Night	Achieve an S Rank in a Sonic the Werehog stage	15
Helping Hand	Complete all townspeople tasks	20
Lay the Smackdown	Master the Stomp technique	10
Wall Crawler	Master the Wall Jump technique	10
Airdevil	Master the Air Boost technique	10
Hyperdrive	Master the Lightspeed Dash technique	10
Basher	Reach Werehog Combat Level 5	10
Smasher	Reach Werehog Combat Level 10	10
Crasher	Reach Werehog Combat Level 15	10

Achievement	How to Earn It	Points
Thrasher	Reach Werehog Combat Level 20	10
Social Butterfly	Talk to all townspeople in the game	30
Hungry Hungry Hedgehog	Collect one of every food type	30
Day Tripper	Clear all Sonic the Hedgehog stages	20
Hard Day's Night	Clear all Sonic the Werehog stages	20
Get on the Exorcise Bandwagon	Exorcise everyone	20
Gyro with Relish	Complete the Apotos Hot Dog stand missions	10
Pig in a Blanket	Complete the Spagonia Hot Dog stand missions	10
Exotic Toppings	Complete the Mazuri Hot Dog stand missions	10
Sausage Fried Rice	Complete the Chun-nan Hot Dog stand missions	10

Achievement	How to Earn It	Points
Iced Hotdog	Complete the Holoska Hot Dog stand missions	10
Kebab on a Bun	Complete the Shamar Hot Dog stand missions	10
Ketchup and Mustard	Complete the Empire City Hot Dog stand missions	10
Fried Clam Roll	Complete the Adabat Hot Dog stand missions	10
Hard Boiled	Complete the Eggmanland Hot Dog stand missions	10
First Time Customer	Buy something from Wentos	10
Oh, You Shouldn't Have!	Give the professor a souvenir	10
That's Enough, Seriously	Give the professor all souvenirs	10
Hedgehunk	Complete the Ana missions in Mazuri and the Louie Montaine missions in Empire City	5
I Ain't Afraid of No Ghost	Complete the Marcantonio missions in Spagonia	5
Blue Meteor	Complete Windmill Isle, Act 2 in 2:35 or less	20
Ace Pilot	Clear Tornado Defense 1 without taking damage	20
BFFs	Be best friends with Chip	20
Speeding Ticket	Complete Arid Sands 1 in 2:50 or less	20
Combo King	Achieve multiple combos	20
Blue Meteor	Dash through white walls at top speed	20
Ring Leader	Gather rings from around the world	20
Knockout Brawler	Smash enemies repeatedly	20

PS3 Trophies

Title	Trophy	How to Earn It
Still Broken	Bronze	Restore the 1st continent
Looking Better	Bronze	Restore the 2nd continent
Still a Jigsaw Puzzle	Bronze	Restore the 3rd continent
Picking Up the Pieces	Bronze	Restore the 4th continent
Almost There	Bronze	Restore the 5th continent
One More to Go	Bronze	Restore the 6th continent
Getting the Hang of Things	Bronze	Achieve an S Rank in a Sonic the Hedgehog stage
Creature of the Night	Bronze	Achieve an S Rank in a Sonic the Werehog stage
Helping Hand	Bronze	Complete all townspeople missions
Lay the Smackdown	Bronze	Master the Stomp technique
Wall Crawler	Bronze	Master the Wall Jump technique
Airdevil	Bronze	Master the Air Boost technique
Hyperdrive	Bronze	Master the Lightspeed Dash technique
Basher	Bronze	Reach Combat Level 5
Smasher	Bronze	Reach Combat Level 10
Crasher	Bronze	Reach Combat Level 15
Thrasher	Bronze	Reach Combat Level 20

Title	Trophy	How to Earn It
Day Tripper	Bronze	Clear all Sonic the Hedgehog stages
Hard Day's Night	Bronze	Clear all Sonic the Werehog stages
Get on the Exorcise Bandwagon	Bronze	Exorcise everyone
Gyro with Relish	Bronze	Complete the Apotos Hot Dog stand missions
Pig in a Blanket	Bronze	Complete the Spagonia Hot Dog stand missions
Exotic Toppings	Bronze	Complete the Mazuri Hot Dog stand missions
Sausage Fried Rice	Bronze	Complete the Chun-nan Hot Dog stand missions
Iced Hotdog	Bronze	Complete the Holoska Hot Dog stand missions
Kebab on a Bun	Bronze	Complete the Shamar Hot Dog stand missions
Ketchup and Mustard	Bronze	Complete the Empire City Hot Dog stand missions
Fried Clam Roll	Bronze	Complete the Adabat Hot Dog stand missions
Hard Boiled	Bronze	Complete the Eggmanland Hot Dog stand missions
First Time Customer	Bronze	Buy something from Wentos
Oh, You Shouldn't Have!	Bronze	Give the professor a souvenir
That's Enough, Seriously	Bronze	Give the professor all souvenirs

Title	Trophy	How to Earn It
Hedgehunk	Bronze	Complete the Ana missions in Mazuri and the Louie Montaine missions in Empire City
I Ain't Afraid of No Ghost	Bronze	Complete the Marcantonio missions in Spagonia
Blue Meteor	Bronze	Complete Windmill Isle, Act 2 in 2:35 or less
Partly Cloudy	Silver	Collect half of the Sun Medals in the game
Sunny	Silver	Collect all Sun Medals
Half Moon	Silver	Collect half of the Moon Medals in the game
Full Moon	Silver	Collect all Moon Medals
Blue Streak	Silver	Max out all Sonic the Hedgehog stats
Power Overwhelming	Silver	Max out all Sonic the Werehog stats
Social Butterfly	Silver	Talk to all townspeople in the game
Hungry Hungry Hedgehog	Silver	Collect one of every food type
Ace Pilot	Silver	Clear Tornado Defense 1 without taking damage
BFFs	Silver	Best friends with Chip
Speeding Ticket	Silver	Complete Arid Sands 1 in 2:50 or less
Combo King	Silver	Achieve 10,000 total combos
Ring Leader	Silver	Collect 5,000 rings
Knockout Brawler	Silver	Defeat 1,000 enemies

A B C D E F G H I J K L M N O P Q R **S** T U V W X Y Z

Title	Trophy	How to Earn It
World Savior	Gold	Clear the Game
100% Clear	Platinum	Collect all the other trophies in the game

SSX BLUR

NINTENDO WII

Peak Tournament Qualifications

Winning tournaments opens up new peak access to your riders, but before you can qualify, you must earn Leaderboard points for credibility. Winning first place in any race will earn you points, but what most riders don't realize is that you can race the same course repeatedly and still tack additional points onto your Leaderboard score. If you're grinding for Leaderboard points, choose your favorite course and stick with it until you have enough points, or go for first in some of the tournamentsyou've already opened. It's the best way reach the new peaks where the snow is steep and deep.

Tourney #1
The Fresh Powder Open
To qualify: 50 points on the Leaderboard

Tourney #2
Yeti's Footsteps
To qualify: 200 points on the Leaderboard
(This tournament opens Peak 2.)

Tourney #3   Amateur Challenge
To qualify: 300 points on the Leaderboard and Peak 2 open

Tourney #4   Eagle's Nest Xtreme
To qualify: 700 points on the Leaderboard and Peak 2 open
(This tournament opens Peak 3.)

Tourney #5   Slopeside Shenanigans
To qualify: 1,000 points on the Leaderboard and Peak 3 open

Tourney #6   Big Air Broadcast
To qualify: 1,200 points on the Leaderboard and Peak 3 open

Tourney #7   Halfpipe Heyday
To qualify: 1,800 points on the Leaderboard and Peak 3 open

Tourney #8   Rat Races
To qualify: 2,100 points on the Leaderboard and Peak 3 open

Tourney #9   Old School Pro Tour
To qualify: 2,500 points on the Leaderboard and Peak 3 open

Tourney #10   Magnum Opus
To qualify: At least a bronze medal in all tournaments

Tourney #11   The Ultra-Super-Secret Platinum Tour
To qualify: Win the Magnum Opus and have a platinum medal

Unlock Luigi and the Grand Finale Galaxy!

Once you have 120 stars and crowns next to the galaxy names on the star map, return to the Comet Observatory and tell Rosalina that you want a rematch with Bowser. After the credits roll, you'll hear a message that Luigi is unlocked.

If you defeat Bowser and earn all 120 stars as Luigi, you'll find the Grand Finale Galaxy at the place where you saw the Star Festival near the beginning of the game. Finish the Grand Finale and you'll find the last star in the game!

SUPER SWING GOLF
NINTENDO WII

Unlock the Caddies!

With the exception of Pipin, caddies can be unlocked in Super Swing Golf by using different characters to complete the PangYa-Festa story. Here are the required conditions:

Caddy	Conditions
Pipin	Complete Tutorial mode
Lola	Complete PangYa-Festa using Uncle Bob
Tiki	Complete PangYa-Festa using Max
Dolfini	Complete PangYa-Festa using Kooh
Quma	Complete PangYa-Festa using Hana
Brie	Complete Pangya-Festa using Arin
TitanBoo	Complete PangYa-Festa using Cecilia

Unlock Other Golfers!

Unlock all the golfers in the game by completing the game using other characters. Here are the required conditions for story mode:

Golfer	Conditions
Uncle Bob	Complete PangYa-Festa using Scout
Cecilia	Complete PangYa-Festa using Hana or Uncle Bob
Max	Complete PangYa-Festa using Cecilia
Kooh	Complete PangYa-Festa using Max
Arin	Complete PangYa-Festa using Kooh
Kaz	Complete Arin's story.

What Do Coins Unlock?

While you're probably used to buying items with coins, Super Swing Golf Season 2 gives you items as you find coins in the game. You keep all of your earnings! Here's the coin count and unlockable items:

Coins	Unlockable Items
84	Gothic Set for Arin, Righteous Rider Set for Max, School Gym Set for Kooh
87	Brie
90	Black Formal Set for Scout, Little Fox Dress-Up Set for Kooh, Pnagya Café Set for Arin
93	Pink Waitress Set for Kooh, Superior Set for Arin
96	Midnight Lola for Lola, Safari Quma for Quma, Sepia Tiki for Tiki
114	Kick Back At Home Set for Kooh
117	Fairy Dress Set for Kooh, Papel Set for Hana, River Battle Set for Kaz
122	Black Lace Brie for Brie, Libera TitanBoo for TitanBoo, Relax at Home Set for Arin, Violet Parka Set for Kaz
141	Hayabusa Ninja for Max, Kasumi Ninja for Arin, Mocchi for Kooh
144	Dark Magable Set for Arin, Simple Tuxedo Set for Kaz
150	Demon Hunter for Cecilia
153	Ayane for Kooh, Tecmobowl for Max

Teenage Mutant Ninja Turtles Gamerscore points

Clean Sweep
50 points
Complete a level without receiving damage. The easiest way to do this is by replaying the first level and using your slam attack to stun your foes before finishing them off. Bad jumps can also hurt, so take your time.

Get Your First Coin
15 points
You can usually knock off this achievement in the first level. Just grab any coin.

Winter's Secret
80 points
Defeat all three of the bosses in Level 16 and win the game. If you're having trouble with the henchmen, take out the archers before clearing the rest of the enemies in the room. Look for a pattern in the platforms leading up to the top of the building.

The Mysterious Leader   76 points
Complete Winter's Tower—level 15 (the second-to-last level in the game). This area has many tough jumps and if you don't have an HDTV, it can be tough to see some obstacles from the shadows. If you're having trouble seeing where to step, pause the game and adjust the contrast or brightness on your television.

Ninjas in the Crypt   72 points
Fight your way through level 14 and Rescue Leo.

All is Forgiven   68 points
Complete level 13. While this level takes place in the city during the day, the jumps and wall moves are difficult in places, so you might need a couple of attempts before you clear all the checkpoints.

Bite me!
64 points
Complete level 12. The jumps in the sewer are numerous and hard to spot in places, so take your time.

O Brother, Where Art Thou   60 points
Fight your way through level 11. This is also the first stage in the game where you can use Raph's special move.

Used Raph's Special Move   30 points
Use Raph's special move in level 11—you must use it at the beginning of the stage to escape from the cell.

When the Slime Comes   56 points
Complete level 10 in the subway maze. Press your A Button whenever your turtle falls into the slime or you'll take damage.

Tower Power   52 points
Complete level 9. Fight your way past enemies using Nightwatcher.

Foot trail
48 points
Complete level 8. You must hurry through this rooftop level or the truck that you're chasing will get away. Run along the easy parts so you'll have more time to concentrate on the difficult jumps.

The Game is the Foot   44 points
Complete level 7. The trick is to measure your jumps so you safely clear the electrical rooftop wires.

Ninja Tag Time   40 points
Complete level 6. You can also earn your Family Unit Gamerscore achievement by pressing the X Button to perform a combination attack.

Family Unit   15 points
Do a combination attack with any other available turtle by pressing the X Button. You can earn this Gamerscore achievement on the dark city rooftops in level 6 of Ninja Tag Time.

Spirit of the Forest   36 points
Complete level 5. This forest area is also where you'll use Leo's special move to unlock another Gamerscore Achievement.

Used Leo's Special Move   30 points
Use Leo's special move to teleport through bars in Spirit of the Forest (level 5).

Cowabunga Carl Getaway   32 points
Complete the fourth level in the game, but watch your step on the rooftops. You'll also use Mike's special move here.

Used Mike's special move   30 points
Use Mike's special move in the Cowabunga Carl Getaway level (level 4).

Techno Ninjutsu　　　　　　　　　　28 points
Complete the third level (the underground sewers) in the game.

Used Don's special move　　　　　　30 points
Use Don's special move in the Techno Ninjutsu level (level 3).

Vigilantism　　　　　　　　　　　24 points
Complete the second level in the game.

Mystical Jungle　　　　　　　　　20 points
Complete the first level in the game. You can try to combine this feat with not taking damage for the Clean Sweep accomplishment, but you might find it easier to figure out the controls and come back to this easy level after you complete the rest of the game.

VIVA PIÑATA
XBOX 360

Turn Sour Piñatas into Residents!
Convert these Sour Piñatas into residents with these tricks:

Sour Piñata	Transform it into a Resident by
Bonboon	Wait for it to lose a fight to a Fourheads piñata.
Cocoadile	Have a garden covering 160 Pinometers and then let the Cocoadile hunt a Sweetooth piñata and two Swanana piñatas.
Crowla	Let it drink a bottle of medicine after you have a birdbath in your garden
Macaraccoon	Let it hunt a Cluckles piñata after you earn five Master Romance awards
Mallowolf	Let it hunt a Pigxie piñata
Profitamole	Using tinkered Toadstools, make two mushrooms in your garden and let it hunt a Profitamole piñata or a Red Flutterscotch piñata
Shellybeen	Let it eat an apple seed
Sherbat	Let it eat a Jack 'O Lantern made from tinkered pumpkins

Viva Piñata Xbox LIVE Gamerscore Achievements

Achievement	How to Earn It	Points
Challenger	Complete five Factory requests	20
Master Challenger	Complete 20 Factory requests	20
Romancer	Rank as a Master Romancer for at least five species	20
Master Romancer	Rank as a Master Collector for at least five species	20
Collector	Have five species take up residence in your garden	20
Master Collector	Have 50 species take up residence in your garden	20
Longevity	Play for 10 hours of real time (not garden time)	20
Garden Value	Own a garden worth 25,000 Chocolate Coins	20

Achievement	How to Earn It	Points
Garden Value Master	Own a garden worth 100,000 Chocolate Coins	20
Piñata Value	Have a piñata worth 5,000 Chocolate Coins	20
Piñata Value Master	Have a piñata worth 10,000 Chocolate Coins	20
Green Fingers	Grow five plants to maturity	20
Master Green Fingers	Grow 25 plants to maturity	20
Wealthy	Earn 25,000 chocolate coins	20
Label Designer	Create a custom label for a piñata	20
Piñata Name Caller	Name a resident piñata	20
Helper Name Caller	Name a helper	20
Talent	Reach level 10	20
Master Talent	Reach level 50	20
Wealth Master	Earn 100,000 Chocolate Coins	20
Land Owner	Expand the size of your garden boundaries once	20
Sour Tower	Create a Tower of Sour with two pieces	20
Sprinkling	Hire a Sprinkling	20
Super Shovel	Unlock all Shovel Head upgrades	20
Taffly Fertilizer	Make fertilizer with a Taffly piñata	20
Master Land Owner	Expand your garden to the maximum size	20
Watchling	Hire a Watchling	20
Diggerling	Hire a Diggerling	20
Shovel Strength	Earn all the Shovel Handle upgrades	20
Weedling	Hire a Weedling	20
Gatherling	Hire a Gatherling	20
Variants	Create five variant piñatas	20

Achievement	How to Earn It	Points
Harvester	Collect produce from Buzzlegum, Moozipan or Goobaa piñatas	20
Master Sour Tower	Create a Tower of Sour with six pieces	20
Generosity	Turn the Beggar into a trader	20
Watering Can Do	Earn all the upgrades for the Watering Can	20
Cluckles Hatches Egg	Hatch an egg using a Cluckles piñata	20
Evolver	Evolve two piñata species	20
Horticulturist	Attain full bonus growth for five plants in your garden	20
Crowla Delay	Distract Dastardos with a Crowla piñata	20
Variants Master	Create 20 piñata variants	20
Pigxie Prize	Cross romance a Swanana piñata with a Rashberry piñata	20

Achievement	How to Earn It	Points
Macaracoon Gift	Have a Macaracoon piñata give you a Romance Sweet	20
Longevity Master	Play the game for at least 50 hours (not garden time)	20
Sherbat Dance	Distract Dastardos using a Sherbat piñata	20
Master Evolver	Evolve eight species	20
Cocoadile Tears	Attain full bonus growth for a plant by using Cocoadile piñata tears	20
Master Horticulturist	Earn full bonus growth for 25 plants	20
Mallowolf Howl	Use the Mallowolf piñata to scare off Ruffians	20
Chewnicorn Healing	Use the power of a Chewnicorn piñata to heal an injured piñata	20

VIVA PIÑATA: TROUBLE IN PARADISE
XBOX 360

Understand Your Gardening Limits!

How many resident piñatas can you have in your garden? That depends on how your garden grows! For the original Viva Piñata and Viva Piñata: Trouble in Paradise, the maximum possible in some gardens is no more than 35, but some players have fewer residents because of their Xbox 360 memory space. If you have fewer than 35 piñatas and the game tells you that your

garden is full, try removing a few trees and other large objects. Big trees and detailed designs eat up extra Xbox 360 memory space. Piñata gardening limits are not limited to exact counts, but by how much memory space is available on the Xbox 360 console, so if you like to decorate your garden with a heaping of clutter, you might find that you can only accommodate 30 resident piñatas. Good to know.

Viva Piñata Trouble in Paradise Xbox LIVE Gamerscore Achievements

Achievement	How to Earn It	Points
Card Sharp	Use a Piñata Card	10
Famous Piñata	Collect a special piñata from a website or trade with someone who has it	20
Records Keeper	Restore ten of Piñata Central's Computer Records	30
Master Exhibitor	Win ten Piñata Shows	20
Desert Collector	Acquire three desert piñata species as garden residents	10
Couch Socialite	Play One-Box Co-op mode for one hour	10
Master Couch Socialite	Play One Box Co-op mode for three hours	20
Region 7 Challenger	Finish all challenges in Region 7	20
Desert Green Fingers	Grow all Desert plants to maturity	20
Arctic Green Fingers	Grow all Arctic plants to maturity	20
Come and Have a Go	Earn a Gold Combat Medal	20

Achievement	How to Earn It	Points
Master Arctic Collector	Acquire all Arctic species as residents	20
Region 2 Challenger	Finish all Challenges in Region 2	20
Packet Bulger	Packet contains all surface types	20
Region 1 Challenger	Finish all of Langston's Destination Challenges in Region 1	20
Full House	Play Four-player Online Co-op mode for one hour	10
Master Card Sharp	Use ten different Piñata Cards	20
SpeedFreak	Win a piñata race	10
Expert Records Keeper	Restore all computer records at Piñata Central	50
Master Records Keeper	Restore 30 records at Piñata Central	40
Exhibitor	Win a piñata show	10
Region 3 Challenger	Finish all of the challenges in Region 3	20
Region 4 Challenger	Finish all of the challenges in Region 4	20
Region 5 Challenger	Finish all of the challenges in Region 5	20
Master Speedfreak	Win ten piñata races	20
Region 6 Challenger	Finish all Challenges in Region 6	20
Master Desert Collector	Acquire all desert piñata species as residents	20
Arctic Collector	Acquire three Arctic piñatas as residents	10
Master Challenger	Finish all Challenges in all regions	50

Unlock the Ski Patrol Uniform!

Star points unlock most clothing and accessories in Wii Ski, but you can only wear the Ski Patrol uniform after you successfully complete a special rescue mission. You must talk to the Ski Patroller at the top of Owl to start this mission. You won't be asked to help unless you complete most of the Ski School assignments (go ahead and complete all of the Ski School stuff because you'll earn a Ski School outfit).

The Ski Patroller will tell you to rescue the skiers stuck in the snow. However, the real challenge here is stopping above the victims so you don't have to sidestep back up the slope. If you plan your route and don't pass anyone by, you should have no problem earning your Ski Patrol uniform.

Edited by Betsy Pringle
Designed by Shane Hartley
Design Production by Kimberly Goddard
Production by Larry Weiner

This edition published by
Scholastic Inc.
New York, NY
www.scholastic.com
Scholastic and associated logos are trademarks of Scholastic Inc.

Scholastic Canada Ltd.; Markham, Ontario

Scholastic Australia Pty. Ltd; Gosford NSW

Scholastic New Zealand Ltd.; Greenmount, Auckland

Grolier International, Inc.
Makati City, Philippines

ISBN-13: 978-0-545-17658-3
ISBN-10: 0-545-17658-1

10 9 8 7 6 5 4 3 2 1

09229
Printed in the United States of America